WHAT IF...?

75 Fascinating
Questions and Answers

WHAT IF...?

75 Fascinating
Questions *and* Answers

The team at HOWSTUFFWORKS.COM

GRAMERCY BOOKS
NEW YORK

This 2007 edition is published by Gramercy Books, an imprint of Random House Value Publishing, by arrangement with Wiley Publishing.

Gramercy is a registered trademark and the colophon is a trademark of Random House, Inc.

Random House
New York • Toronto • London • Sydney • Auckland
www.valuebooks.com

A catalog record for this title is available from the Library of Congress.

ISBN: 978-0-517-22984-2

Printed and bound in the United States of America

10 9 8 7 6 5 4 3 2 1

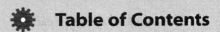 **Table of Contents**

What if I accidentally super-glued my fingers or lips together?

What if I had earrings or some other body piercing and forgot to remove the jewelry before I had an MRI?

What if I wanted to visit all seven continents in one day? Is this possible?

What if I were on a roller coaster going through a loop-the-loop and my safety harness broke?

What if two people stumbled into quicksand — would the heavier person sink faster?

What if I were on an elevator and the cable broke?

What if I accidentally zapped someone with my stun gun?

What if I accidentally ended up locked in a walk-in freezer?

What if I were stranded several miles off shore in cold weather?

What if I were ice fishing and fell through the ice?

What if someone picked my pocket or stole my wallet?

What if I got to be a contestant on one of those survival game shows and I had to walk on fire or lay on a bed of nails?

What if my SCUBA diving equipment failed?

Hello!

One of the fascinating things about HowStuffWorks is what it does to your brain. You look at the things around you differently when you know how they work, and you also ask more questions about them. As you learn how more and more things work, something else happens too — it just seems like you naturally start asking "what if?" questions.

Things that start popping into your head are questions like "What if I combine this with that?" or "What will happen if this trend continues?" or "What if a certain technology fails instead of working like it is supposed to?" In a lot of cases, the more you learn, the more questions you have! You'd think it would be the other way around, but it's not. . . .

In this book, I've taken a bunch of "what if?" questions that popped into my head and answered them using the HowStuffWorks method. The goal is to learn about the technology and the side effects, and see how it all fits together. The result can be something creative — "What if we tried to build a domed city?" — or destructive — "What if the Hoover Dam crumbles?" — but the results are always interesting!

As you look through the book, you will notice two icons:

 One is the MB icon. The questions that are marked with this icon are my personal favorites. These are the questions that just got more and more interesting the more I thought about them.

 And the other is the VR icon — the visitor's request icon. This icon identifies the questions that our visitors picked to be the most intriguing of the questions in the table of contents.

If you find that this collection of questions sparks other questions in your own mind, send them along — I'd love to hear them. Visit the HowStuffWorks Web site and enter them in the "What If?" forum. The questions in this forum will form the foundation of the next book!

WHAT IF...?

75 Fascinating
Questions *and* Answers

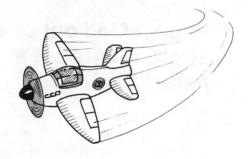

1

Air and Space

✻ What if I fell out of an airplane without a parachute? • What if someone shot a gun on an airplane? • What if an asteroid hit the earth? • What if an astronaut went on a spacewalk without wearing a spacesuit? • What if an astronaut took his or her pet bird into space? Would it still be able to fly? • What if I went to Mars for a year to study the planet — how much food and water would I have to take with me to survive? • What if we wanted to build a colony on the moon? • What if we were next to a black hole?

What if I fell out of an airplane without a parachute?

You know it's going to be a bad day when you find yourself falling through the air without a parachute! But let's say that, somehow, you were to fall out of an airplane and find yourself in that exact situation.

The first thing to keep in mind is that you have to think fast. If you fall out at 12,000 feet (about 2.2 miles or 3.6 km up), you only have about 60 seconds before you hit the ground. In free fall, you fall at about 125 miles per hour (200 kph) if you have your arms and legs extended, and at that speed you will travel about 12,000 feet in one minute.

The first thing to do is to look for a body of water. Diving into water won't feel good at 125 mph, but you will survive if the water is deep enough — at least 12 feet deep or so. Steer toward the water (it's helpful if you've been skydiving before and know how to steer as you're falling) and dive right in. If you don't know how deep it is, go feet first just in case.

If there's no water around, then you need to try something else. One person in World War II survived a jump without a parachute from about 18,000 feet. He fell through the branches in a pine thicket and landed in deep snow. So you might try looking for some trees and hope for the best.

Lacking water or trees — for example, you're falling in an urban area and can't spot a rooftop pool — your next option is to look for something big with the hope that it will break your fall. Landing on the roof of an RV, a mobile home, or a truck's trailer is a possibility. These structures are not extremely strong. When you hit them, they will break and absorb some of the energy of the fall. Whether it will be enough energy or not is an open question. There's only one way to find out — but we don't recommend trying it.

What if someone shot a gun on an airplane?

There are lots of scenes in movies where terrorists or hijackers take over an airplane and start shooting up the place. There's even the movie *Air Force One*, where the president is shooting a gun and the terrorists are shooting back. Is this possible? Wouldn't the plane explode or depressurize as soon as the bullet hit the skin of the airplane?

There are four things that might happen if a person were to fire a gun on an airplane:

- The bullet simply goes through the aluminum skin of the plane and punches a small hole as it exits.
- The bullet hits a window and blows it out.
- The bullet hits wiring hidden in the walls or the floor.
- The bullet hits a fuel tank.

If a bullet simply punctures the skin of an airplane, then it's no big deal. The cabin of the airplane is pressurized and the hole creates a small leak, but the pressurization system will compensate for it. A single hole, or even a few holes like this, will have no effect.

If the bullet blows out a window, that's a problem. When the window blows, the plane will depressurize over the course of several seconds. Since all of the air in the cockpit is rushing toward the missing window, a lot of debris will be heading in that direction with it. If the person sitting next to the window isn't strapped in, then it's possible that he or she will get sucked out — another good reason to wear your safety belt at all times!

In the meantime, the loss of cabin pressurization creates a problem for everyone on the plane. A commercial airliner flying at 30,000 feet is flying slightly higher than the peak of Mt. Everest. The air at this altitude is so thin that a person will become incoherent in a matter of a minute or so without supplemental oxygen. That's why oxygen masks will drop from the panel in the ceiling. If you're in this situation, putting the mask on quickly, while you're still thinking clearly, is important.

If the bullet hits wiring (or worse, if the bullet hits something important like the instrument panel in the cockpit), it could cause problems that range from trivial (in-flight entertainment stops working) to severe. The damage depends on what gets hits and how important it is.

Finally, there's the problem of the fuel tanks. Commercial jets store a lot of their fuel in the wings, but there are also tanks in the fuselage on many planes. For example, a 747 stores thousands of gallons of fuel in the fuselage. If a bullet were to puncture a tank, it would at least cause a leak and would have some potential to cause an explosion.

From this discussion, you can see that, in general, it's not a good idea to be shooting guns on airplanes! But if you have to do it, try not to hit anything important.

What if an asteroid hit the earth?

An asteroid striking our planet — it's the stuff of science fiction. Many movies and books have portrayed this possibility (*Deep Impact, Armageddon, Lucifer's Hammer,* and so on).

An asteroid impact is also the stuff of science fact. There are obvious craters on the earth (and the moon) that show us a long history of large objects hitting the planet. The most famous asteroid ever is the one that landed on earth 65 million years ago. It is thought that this asteroid threw so much moisture and dust into the atmosphere that it cut off sunlight, lowering temperatures worldwide and causing the extinction of the dinosaurs.

So what if an asteroid were to hit the earth today?

Any asteroid falling from the sky would have a tremendous amount of energy. Here is a typical example. In 2028, the asteroid 1997XF11 will come extremely close to earth but will miss the planet. If something were to change and it did hit the earth, what you would have is a mile-wide asteroid striking the planet's surface at about 30,000 mph. An asteroid that big traveling at that speed has the energy roughly equal to a 1 million megaton bomb. It is very likely that an asteroid like this would wipe out most of the life on the planet.

It is difficult to imagine 1 million megatons, so let's try some smaller sizes. Let's say that an asteroid the size of a house crashed on earth at 30,000 miles per hour. It would have an amount of energy roughly equal to the bomb that fell on Hiroshima — perhaps 20 kilotons. An asteroid like this would flatten reinforced concrete buildings up to half a mile from ground zero, and flatten wooden structures perhaps a mile and a half from ground zero. It would, in other words, do extensive damage to any city.

If the asteroid is as big as a 20-story building (200 feet on a side), it has an amount of energy equal to the largest nuclear bombs made today — on the order of 25 to 50 megatons. An asteroid like this would flatten reinforced concrete buildings 5 miles from ground zero. It would completely destroy most major cities in the U.S.

By the time you get up to a mile-wide asteroid, you are working in the 1 million megaton range. This asteroid has energy that is 10 million times greater than the bomb that fell on Hiroshima. It is able to flatten everything for 100 to 200 miles out from ground zero. In other words, if a mile-wide asteroid were to directly hit New York City, the force of the impact probably would completely flatten every single thing from Washington D.C. to Boston, and would cause extensive damage perhaps 1,000 miles out — that's as far away as Chicago. The amount of dust and debris thrown up into the atmosphere would block out the sun and cause most living things on the planet to perish. If an asteroid that big were to land in the ocean, it would cause massive tidal waves hundreds of feet high that would completely scrub the coastlines in the vicinity.

In other words, if an asteroid strikes the earth, it will be a really, really bad day no matter how big it is. If the asteroid is a mile in diameter, it's likely to wipe out life on the planet. Let's hope it doesn't happen anytime soon!

What if an astronaut went on a spacewalk without wearing a spacesuit?

The current spacesuit that is used for spacewalking from the shuttle and International Space Station is called the

Extravehicular Mobility Unit, or EMU. Because an earth-like environment is created within the suit itself, a spacesuit allows you to walk around in space in relative safety. Spacesuits provide

- Pressurized atmosphere — The spacesuit provides air pressure to keep the fluids in your body in a liquid state — in other words, to prevent your bodily fluids from boiling. The pressure in the suit is much lower than normal air pressure on earth (4.3 versus 14.7 psi) so that the suit doesn't balloon and so that it is as flexible as possible.

- Oxygen — Spacesuits must supply pure oxygen, because of the low pressure. Normal air — 78% nitrogen, 21% oxygen, and 1% other gases — would cause dangerously low oxygen concentrations in the lungs and blood at this low pressure.

- Regulated temperature — To cope with the extremes of temperature in space, most spacesuits are heavily insulated with layers of fabric (Neoprene, Gore-Tex, Dacron) and covered with reflective outer layers (Mylar or white fabric) to reflect sunlight.

- Protection from micrometeoroids — Spacesuits have multiple layers of durable fabrics such as Dacron or Kevlar. These layers prevent the suit from tearing on exposed surfaces of the spacecraft.

Outer space is an extremely hostile place. If you were to step outside a spacecraft such as the International Space Station or onto a world with little or no atmosphere, such as the moon or Mars, and you weren't wearing a spacesuit, here's what would happen:

- You would become unconscious within 15 seconds because there is no oxygen.

- Your blood and body fluids would boil and then freeze, because there's little or no air pressure.

- Your tissues (skin, heart, other internal organs) would expand because of the boiling fluids.

- You would face extreme changes in temperature:
  - Sunlight: 248° Fahrenheit (120° Celsius)
  - Shade: −148°F (−100°C)

- You would be exposed to various types of radiation, such as cosmic rays, and charged particles emitted from the sun (solar wind).
- You could be hit by small particles of dust or rock that move at high speeds (micrometeoroids) or orbiting debris from satellites or spacecraft.

The human body could tolerate a complete vacuum for a few seconds at the most. So the scene in *2001: A Space Odyssey* where Dave ejects from the pod into the vacuum of space and dives for the space station — that might actually work. But beyond a few seconds, things would get ugly fast.

What if an astronaut took his or her pet bird into space? Would it still be able to fly?

The coolest part about a spaceship or space station orbiting the earth is the weightlessness. It's cool to humans because in weightlessness anyone can fly. You simply kick off of a wall and you can fly in a straight line to the other side of the ship without any effort. If you've seen video of astronauts clowning around on the space shuttle or in the space station, then you know that it looks like a lot of fun!

So what would a bird do in the space station? No one has ever really tried it, probably because of the hygiene problems. But if you had a big open space in the space station and released a bird into it, what would the bird do?

Think about what a bird does on earth. It flaps its wings a lot to take off, it flaps its wings while it is flying to stay in the air, and then it flaps its wings a lot when it lands to decelerate. Some birds, like hawks, are extremely good at gliding. They can stay in the air for long periods of time without any flapping once they are airborne.

In space, a bird would need to do the same sorts of things at both ends of the flight. It would need to flap a lot at the beginning to build up some speed, and it would need to flap a lot at the end to

7

slow down (or it could do what humans do at the end of their weightless flights and run into a wall). In the middle of the flight, the bird would simply glide. It doesn't have to expend any energy during the flight because gravity is not pulling it down.

The big advantage that a bird would have over human beings in this situation is its wings. Inside a space station full of air, the bird's wings and tail would still work fine. So the bird can turn, accelerate, and decelerate mid-flight. Humans cannot do this — once a human kicks off the wall, the flight is pretty much a straight line until the human hits the opposite wall. Birds would have a tremendous amount of control while flying in the space station if they used their wings and tails properly, although they would have to make some serious adjustments to compensate for their weightlessness.

The lingering, unknown question is this: is a bird smart enough to adjust to things in a zero-gravity environment? Or is flying in gravity so instinctive that a bird cannot adjust? Birds are remarkably smart, so chances are that a domesticated bird would figure it out with a little practice.

What if I went to Mars for a year to study the planet — how much food and water would I have to take with me to survive?

Another way to phrase this question would be to ask, "How much does a person eat in two years?" A trip to Mars is supposed to take six months to get there and six months to get back. So if you plan to stay a year on the planet to conduct your research, you're looking at a total of two years for your interplanetary trek.

A typical male who weighs 200 pounds and is getting some exercise needs the following on a daily basis:

- 2,500 calories
- 83 grams of fat
- 60 grams of protein

- 25 grams of fiber
- A wide assortment of vitamins and minerals

A typical woman would require less of everything, so this way we know we're covered.

We can assume that the food can be supplemented with vitamins and minerals (either mixed in or as tablets), so there's no need to worry about that part of the equation. The whole problem comes down to calories, protein, fat, and fiber.

If you want to be a minimalist about it, you can get your calories from white sugar, your fat from vegetable oil, your protein from protein powder, and your fiber from bran. In this case, each person on the two-year journey would need

- 274 kilograms (602 pounds) of sugar
- 60 kilograms (133 pounds) of vegetable oil
- 43 kilograms (96 pounds) of protein
- 18 kilograms (40 pounds) of fiber

If you formed all of those ingredients into bars or kibble, you would need about 400 kilograms, or 880 pounds, of food per person. When you buy dog food at the grocery store, a typical large bag holds 20 pounds. So you would need 44 large dog-food-sized bags to keep one person alive for two years.

The other thing a person needs is water. On most space missions, water is a by-product of electricity production in fuel cells, so it is not a big concern. Nutritionists recommend that you drink at least eight 8-ounce glasses of water a day. Let's say you might be a tad thirstier. So for a two-year mission a person would need about 456 gallons of water.

What if we wanted to build a colony on the moon?

Anyone who grew up with the Apollo moon launches in the 1970s, along with the movie *2001: A Space Odyssey* (which premiered in 1968), was left with the impression that colonies would be on the moon ANY DAY NOW. Given that it's now 30 years later and there has been no significant progress, it's safe to assume that there won't be a moon colony any time soon. But it's still a tantalizing thought. Wouldn't it be cool to be able to live, vacation, and work on the moon?

Let's say we did want to colonize the moon. There are some basic needs that the moon colonists would have to take care of if this were any sort of long-term living arrangement. The most basic fundamentals include

- Breathable air
- Water
- Food
- Pressurized shelter
- Power

It would be ideal to get as many of these resources as possible from the moon itself, because shipping costs to the moon are unbelievable — something on the order of $50,000 per pound. Just 1 gallon of water weighs about 8 pounds, so it costs $400,000 to get it to the moon! At those rates, you want to carry as little as possible to the moon and manufacture as much as you can once you get there.

Obtaining breathable air, in the form of oxygen, is fairly easy on the moon. The soil on the moon contains oxygen, which can be harvested using heat and electricity.

Water is trickier. There is now some evidence that there may be water on the moon, in the form of buried ice that has collected at the south pole. If so, water mining might be possible, and it would solve a lot of problems. Water is necessary for drinking and irrigation, and it can also be converted to hydrogen and oxygen for use as rocket fuel.

If water is not available on the moon, it must be imported from earth. One way to do that would be to ship liquid hydrogen from the earth to the moon, and then react it with oxygen from the moon's soil to create water. Since water molecules are 67% oxygen and 33% hydrogen by weight, this might be the cheapest way to get water to the moon. As a side benefit, the hydrogen can react with oxygen in a fuel cell to create electricity as it creates water.

Food is also a problem. One person eats about 450 pounds of dehydrated food per year. A whole colony of people would require tons of food. The first thought that anyone on earth would have is "Grow the food on the moon." We think that way because here on earth chemicals like carbon and nitrogen are freely available in the atmosphere, and minerals are freely available in the earth's soil. A ton of wheat is made up of a ton of carbon, nitrogen, oxygen, hydrogen, potassium, phosphorous, and so on. To grow a ton of wheat on the moon, you will have to import all the chemicals not readily available on the moon. Once the first crop is in, and as long as the colony's population is stable, then the chemicals can be reused in a natural cycle. The plant grows, a person eats it, and the person excretes it as solid waste, liquid waste, and carbon dioxide in the breath. These waste products then nourish the next batch of plants. But you still have to get tons of food or chemicals to the moon to start the cycle.

In the shelter category, it's likely that the first shelters will be inflatable structures imported from earth, but a lot of research has been done on the possibility of building structures from ceramics and metals created on the moon.

Power on the moon is an interesting challenge. It would probably be possible to manufacture solar cells on the moon, but sunlight is available only part of the time. As mentioned previously, hydrogen and oxygen can react in a fuel cell to create electricity. Nuclear power is another possibility, using uranium mined on the moon.

With all of this information, you can begin to see why there isn't a colony on the moon right now — it's complicated! But let's imagine that we wanted to create a 100-person, self-sustaining colony on the moon. Let's further imagine that, to start the colony, the following was shipped to the moon per person:

- The person him/herself — 200 pounds
- A starter pack of food (or chemicals to grow food) — 500 pounds per person
- Initial shelter and equipment — 1,000 pounds
- Manufacturing equipment — 1,000 pounds

That's approximately 3,000 pounds per person, and 300,000 pounds for the colony. When you realize that the space shuttle orbiter weighs 165,000 pounds without fuel, and you understand that the 100 people are going to live their entire lives on the moon off of the materials found in just two space shuttle orbiters, you realize how extremely optimistic this weight estimate is. At

$50,000 per pound, that's $15 billion just for the shipping costs. By the time you factor in design, development, materials, training, people, and administrative costs, as well as the actual amounts of materials that have to be sent, as well as the time and money that has been invested just to get the International Space Station into low-earth orbit, you can see that even a small colony on the moon would cost hundreds of billions, if not trillions, of dollars.

Maybe next year. . . .

What if we were next to a black hole?

To answer this question, first we need to look at what black holes are and how they work. A black hole is what remains when a massive star dies. A massive star usually has a core that is at least three times the mass of the sun. Stars are huge, amazing fusion reactors. Because stars are so large and are made out of gas, an intense gravitational field is always trying to collapse the star. The fusion reactions happening in the core are like a giant fusion bomb that is trying to explode the star. The balance between the gravitational forces and the explosive forces is what defines the size of the star.

As the star dies, the nuclear fusion reactions stop because the fuel for these reactions gets used up. At the same time, the star's gravity pulls material inward and compresses the core. As the core compresses, it heats up and eventually creates a supernova explosion in which the material and radiation blast out into space. What remains is the highly compressed, and extremely massive, core.

This object is now a black hole. It literally disappears from view. Because the core's gravity is so strong, the core sinks through the fabric of space-time, creating a hole in space-time. What was the core of the original star now becomes the central part of the black hole — it's called the *singularity*. The opening of the hole is called the *event horizon*.

You can think of the event horizon as the mouth of the black hole. Once something passes the event horizon, it is gone for good. Once inside the event horizon, all *events* (points in space-time) stop, and nothing — not even light — can escape.

There are two types of black holes:

- The Schwarzschild black hole is the simplest black hole, in which the core does not rotate. This type of black hole only has a singularity and an event horizon.
- The Kerr black hole, which is probably the more common form in nature, rotates because the star from which it was formed was rotating. When the rotating star collapses, the core continues to rotate, and this carries over to the black hole. The Kerr black hole has the following parts:
  - Singularity — the collapsed core
  - Event horizon — the opening of the hole
  - Ergosphere — an egg-shaped region of distorted space around the event horizon (caused by the spinning of the black hole, which "drags" the space around it)
  - Static limit — the boundary between the ergosphere and normal space

Black holes will not consume everything around them. If an object passes into the ergosphere, it can still be ejected from the black hole by gaining energy from the hole's rotation. However, if an object crosses the event horizon, it will be sucked into the black hole and never escape. What happens inside the black hole is unknown.

So, what if the sun were to become a black hole? It turns out that the chances of this actually happening are pretty much nil. The sun's core isn't large enough for it to become a black hole at all. When the sun dies, about 5 billion or so years from now, scientists believe it will expand into a red giant. As this happens, the sun will increase in size and most likely consume Mercury and Venus and possibly Earth. Eventually, millions of years later, the sun will quite literally run out of gas. When this happens, a planetary nebula will form, leaving behind a very dense, mostly carbon core about the size of the earth. At this point, the sun will be a white dwarf. As its temperature continues to cool it will eventually become a black dwarf.

Now, just for argument's sake, suppose the sun did become a black hole and the Earth and other planets managed to survive the transformation. Since the sun is a rotating star, its core would continue to rotate, making it a Kerr black hole with an ergosphere. Because the sun's core is very small, the ergosphere would also be small — so small, in fact, that the planets would probably just continue to orbit in their usual manner. The black hole would have the same mass, and therefore the same gravity, as the original sun. Orbiting planets wouldn't notice any difference.

Obviously, if this were to happen, life as we know it would be changed dramatically — but for a different reason. A black hole emits no light. Darkness would engulf the earth, and it would be extremely cold. The oceans would probably freeze, and any existing life forms would die off rather guickly. If humans could get underground with a good way to generate electricity and heat, they might survive. But it would be pretty bleak out on the surface.

2

Land and Sea

✹ What if the polar ice caps melted? · What if people wanted to use icebergs as a source of fresh water? · What if a plane were landing at the airport in San Francisco and there was a big earthquake? · What if the Alaska pipeline blew up? · What if the Hoover Dam broke? · What if a wildfire came near my house? · What if a main water supply gets infected with some form of bacteria? · What if I wanted to build a Great Pyramid today? How much would it cost? · What if we covered a city in a giant glass dome? · What if the U.S. put all its trash in one giant landfill? · What if there were no gravity on earth? What if gravity doubled?

What if the polar ice caps melted?

You've probably heard the term *global warming*. It seems that in the last hundred years the earth's temperature has increased about half a degree Celsius. This may not sound like much, but even half a degree can have a big effect on our planet. According to the U.S. Environmental Protection Agency, the sea level has risen 6 to 8 inches (15 to 20 cm) in the last hundred years.

This higher temperature may be causing some floating icebergs to melt. However, it's not really the melted water that's making the oceans rise. Think of a glass of water that is filled halfway. You drop a few ice cubes into it and the water level rises; the more you add, the more the water level rises. Icebergs are large, floating chunks of ice that break off from landmasses and fall into the ocean. In other words, icebergs are like really big ice cubes floating in a really big glass of water. The rising temperature may be causing more icebergs to form by weakening glaciers, causing more cracks and making ice more likely to break off. As soon as the ice falls into the ocean, the ocean rises a little.

If the rising temperature affects glaciers and icebergs, could the polar ice caps be in danger of melting and causing the oceans to rise? This could happen, but no one knows when it might happen.

The main ice-covered landmass is Antarctica at the South Pole, with about 90% of the world's ice (and 70% of its fresh water). Antarctica is covered with ice an average of 7,000 feet (2,133 meters) thick. If all of the Antarctic ice melted, sea levels around the world would rise about 200 feet (61 meters). But the average temperature in Antarctica is −37°C, so the ice there is in no danger of melting. In fact, in most parts of the continent the temperature never gets above freezing.

At the other end of the world, the North Pole, the ice is not nearly as thick as at the South Pole. The ice floats on the Arctic Ocean. If it melted, sea levels would not be affected.

There is a significant amount of ice covering Greenland, which would add another 20 feet (7 meters) to the oceans if it melted. Because Greenland is closer to the equator than Antarctica, the temperatures there are higher, so the ice is more likely to melt.

But there might be a less dramatic reason for the higher ocean level than polar ice melting — the higher temperature of the water. Water is most dense at 4°C. Above and below this temperature, the density of water decreases (the same weight of water occupies a bigger space). So as the overall temperature of water increases, it naturally expands a little bit, making the oceans rise.

In 1995 the International Panel on Climate Change issued a report that contained various projections of sea level change by the year 2100. It estimates that the sea will rise 20 inches (50 centimeters) with the lowest estimates at 6 inches (15 centimeters) and the highest at 37 inches (95 centimeters). The rise will come from thermal expansion of the ocean and from melting glaciers and ice sheets. Twenty inches is no small amount — it could have a big effect on coastal cities, especially during storms.

What if people wanted to use icebergs as a source of fresh water?

Fresh water is scarce in many parts of the world. Places like Southern California, Saudi Arabia, and many countries on the African continent can use all the fresh water they can get. Something like 70% of the earth's fresh water is locked up in the polar ice caps, and the ice caps calve icebergs naturally all the time. It therefore makes sense to think about towing huge icebergs to the places in the world that need fresh water the most.

It would be great if you could easily transport an iceberg. A good-sized iceberg might measure 3,000 x 1,500 x 600 feet. An iceberg that size contains somewhere around 20 billion gallons of fresh water. If 1 million people each use 10 gallons of water a day, then 20 billion gallons of water would take care of the water needs of 1 million people for over 5 years. For 10 million people, it would last 200 days. It really is a lot of water.

The first question is: Can you do it? With today's technology, it certainly is possible from a brute force standpoint. You can hunt for big, stable icebergs using satellites, attach tugboats to them, and drag them anywhere. However, there are two problems that you have to solve to make it work.

The first problem is melting. If you've ever run tap water over an ice cube, you know that even cold running water can melt an ice cube very quickly. It's the same effect that causes wind chill, but with running water the effect is even greater. If you were to try towing a naked iceberg to Southern California, it would melt long before it got there. Therefore, you have to wrap some sort of covering around the iceberg to insulate it a little. You might even want the wrapper to hold in the melted water so that you don't lose any water along the way. Obviously, a covering that big uses a LOT of fabric, and even if it's made from extremely strong Kevlar, there's a chance it could rip in a storm.

The second problem is the draft of an iceberg. The expression "tip of the iceberg" comes from the fact that almost all of an iceberg is submerged under the water. A big iceberg is hundreds of feet deep. The size will make it hard to get it anywhere near land. It will have to melt in its fabric wrapper well offshore, and then the water can be pumped in.

To solve both of these problems, it might be easier to mine the icebergs in the Arctic and fill up supertankers with ice shavings. Modern supertankers can hold something like 100 million gallons of liquid. That's a drop in the bucket compared to the 20 billion gallons in an iceberg, but it would be a lot quicker and easier to move it around in a supertanker. Since fresh water doesn't pose nearly the environmental hazard that oil does, it might be possible to build much larger ships that hold far more liquid.

Either way, you will hear more and more about fresh water in the years to come. As the human population grows, water will become a critical resource in many parts of the world.

What if a plane were landing at the airport in San Francisco, and just as it touched down, there was a big earthquake?

An earthquake is one of the most terrifying phenomena that nature can dish up. We generally think of the ground we stand on as rock solid and completely stable. An earthquake can shatter that perception instantly, and often with extreme violence. Let's take a look at how earthquakes work in order to understand what could be happening as the plane touches down.

An earthquake is a vibration that travels through the earth's crust. Technically, a large truck that rumbles down the street is causing a mini-earthquake if you feel your house shaking as it goes by. But we tend to think of earthquakes as events that affect a fairly large area, such as an entire city. Although all kinds of things can cause earthquakes — such as volcanic eruptions or underground explosions — the majority of naturally occurring earthquakes are caused by movements of the earth's plates. The study of this type of plate movement is called *plate tectonics.*

Scientists proposed the idea of plate tectonics to explain a number of peculiar phenomenon on earth, such as the apparent movement of continents over time, the clustering of volcanic activity in certain areas, and the presence of huge ridges at the bottom of the ocean. The basic theory is that the surface layer of the earth — the lithosphere — is made up of many plates that slide over the lubricating athenosphere layer. Where these plates meet, you'll find faults — breaks in the earth's crust where the blocks of rock on each side are moving in different directions.

Earthquakes are much more common along fault lines than they are anywhere else on the planet. One of the best-known faults is the San Andreas fault in California. This fault, which marks the plate boundary between the Pacific oceanic plate and the North American continental plate, extends across 650 miles (1,050 km) of land. San Francisco, along with it's new international airport, is very close to this fault.

When a sudden break or shift occurs in the earth's crust, the energy radiates out as seismic waves, just as the energy from a disturbance in a body of water radiates out in wave form. Surface waves, which are one form of seismic waves, act something like the waves in a body of water — they move the surface of the earth up and down and cause a great deal of damage.

In some areas, severe earthquake damage is the result of liquefaction of soil. In the right conditions, the violent shaking from an earthquake will make loosely packed sediments and soil behave like a liquid. When a building or house is built on this type of sediment, liquefaction will cause the structure to collapse more easily. During the Loma Prieta earthquake, the Oakland

International Airport's main runway suffered severe damage due to liquefaction — cracks measuring up to 3 feet wide were found.

To help it withstand earthquakes, the new San Francisco International Airport uses a bunch of advanced building technologies. One of these technologies involves giant ball bearings.

As you can see, airports located in earthquake prone areas have several safety issues to consider, such as:

- The integrity of the buildings and terminals
- The integrity of the control tower
- The integrity of the runways

The 267 columns that support the weight of the airport each ride on a 5-foot-diameter steel ball bearing. The ball rests in a concave base that is connected to the ground. In the event of an earthquake, the ground can move 20 inches in any direction. The columns that rest on the balls move somewhat less than this as they roll around in their bases, which helps isolate the building from the motion of the ground. When the earthquake is over, gravity pulls the columns back to the center of their bases. This takes care of the folks waiting for a departing flight, but what about the people that are on arriving flights?

As we've mentioned, runways can suffer some pretty serious damage due to liquefaction, so a plane landing just after an earthquake could have quite a treacherous runway to maneuver. If the people in the control tower feel the earthquake and can radio the pilot, the plane could divert and avoid landing at all. But if a plane happens to be landing just as the first shock of an earthquake hits, it's not a big problem. The plane's landing gear is designed to handle big shocks from hard landings, so you can ride out the earthquake in comfort.

What if the Alaska pipeline blew up?

The Alaska pipeline is an amazing structure that carries oil from wells in the very far north of Alaska down to the ice-free port in Valdez, Alaska, where tankers pick up and transport the oil. The pipeline is 800 miles long and 4 feet in diameter. Sometimes it is above ground and sometimes below, and in the process it crosses over 800 rivers and streams.

More than one million barrels of crude oil move through the pipeline each day. At 42 gallons per barrel, that means that the pipeline supplies about 6% of the oil used in the United States.

What happened when a hunter hit the pipeline

You can get some sense of what would happen if the Alaska pipeline blew up by looking at a microcosmic event that occurred in October 2001. A hunter, apparently inebriated, shot the pipeline with a hunting rifle and punctured it. A bullet would not make a very big hole — maybe the size of a dime. Because of the pressure inside the pipeline, however, 120 gallons of oil per minute sprayed out of the hole. Over the course of 36 hours, the pipeline was shut down and the oil had to be drained from the punctured section so that it could be repaired. But in that 36 hours, over 300,000 gallons of oil sprayed onto the trees and ground around the puncture, creating a massive spill.

If someone were to blow up the pipeline, it would make the mess from a tiny bullet hole look like a pinprick. Assume that officials reacted quickly after the blast, shut down the pipeline, closed valves to block back-flowing oil, and had everything under control in 24 hours. Something like 40 million gallons of oil would be lying on the ground. That's enough oil to fill 40,000 swimming pools. Or enough to nearly fill an entire supertanker like the Exxon Valdez. Or to cover 100 acres of land in oil over a foot deep.

It would be even worse if the leak occurred near a river because the oil would flow into the river and then downstream, destroying the river along the way.

Simply speaking, it would be a real mess. It took over $2 billion to clean up the 11 million gallons that leaked from the Exxon Valdez. The advantage of a spill at sea is that much of the oil stays at sea and never makes it to land. In the case of the pipeline, you would possibly have almost four times the oil all in one place — and it would all be on land. The oil would run off to the local streams and rivers, just like rainwater does, destroying all the wildlife in its path.

What if the Hoover Dam broke?

The Hoover Dam is one of those miracles of the modern world that almost defy explanation. When you stand next to it, the size is unbelievable. It is over 700 feet high (imagine a 70-story building). The top of the dam is over 1,200 feet long. At the base it is an amazing 660 feet thick and at the top it is 45 feet thick. The water on the lake side is over 500 feet deep, and the lake holds a total of 10 trillion or so gallons of water — enough water to cover the state of Connecticut 10 feet deep.

Let's say the Hoover Dam broke. This is difficult to imagine, given its thickness. No conventional bomb would have an effect on a dam like this. It's difficult to imagine even a nuclear bomb having an effect, unless it were an extremely powerful one and it were inside the dam at the time of explosion. But let's say that some sort of tremendous earthquake or an asteroid strike or some other natural disaster were to somehow eliminate the Hoover Dam in one fell swoop. What would happen?

The first thing that would happen is that 10 trillion gallons of water would move as quickly as it could out of the lake and down the river in a huge tsunami of water. The Hoover Dam is located in a desert area that is not hugely inhabited below the dam, but there are still some sizeable populations. Lake Havasu City, population 40,000, is about the biggest town along the river. Bullhead City, population 30,000, is also close to the dam. Needles, California; Blythe, California; and Laughlin, Nevada, all have populations of around 10,000 people as well.

Where the water would do immense damage is in the lakes below Hoover Dam. It turns out that below Hoover Dam is another large lake called Lake Mohave, which is held in place by Davis Dam, and below that is Lake Havasu, held in place by Parker Dam. These are smaller lakes and smaller dams. For example, Lake Havasu only holds about 200 billion gallons of water.

As the water released by the Hoover Dam moved through these two lakes, it would likely destroy them and their dams as well. That's where the real impact would be felt, because these lakes affect a huge number of people. The water in them produces hydroelectric power, irrigates farmland, and supplies drinking water to cities like Los Angeles, Las Vegas, Phoenix, and San Diego.

The Hoover Dam produces roughly 2,000 megawatts of power. Davis and Parker Dams produce less, but together they might all produce 3,000 megawatts. That represents about one half of one percent of the total electrical power produced in the United States. If you eliminated a sizable amount of generating capacity like that, especially in that area of the country (near Los Angeles and Las Vegas), it would definitely cause problems.

The destruction of irrigation water supplies would also have a huge effect on farming in the region. Farmers in the Imperial Valley get most of their water from the Colorado River, and these irrigation systems would collapse. Prior to irrigation, the Imperial Valley was a barren desert. Today it is the home of over half a million acres of farmland and produces over a billion dollars in fruits and vegetables every year.

There would be large effects as well from the loss of drinking water. For example, Las Vegas gets 85% of its drinking water from Lake Mead — the lake behind Hoover Dam. With the loss of water and the loss of power, Las Vegas would become uninhabitable, and that would displace 1.5 million residents and empty over 120,000 hotels rooms as well as the casinos, bringing the multi-billion-dollar gambling industry in this city to a halt.

Isn't it amazing how much commerce, and how many people, depend on that one dam?

What if a wildfire came near my house?

In just seconds, a spark, or even the sun's heat alone, can set off an inferno. Wildfires spread quickly, consuming thick, dried-out vegetation and almost everything else in their path. What was once a forest becomes a virtual powder keg of untapped fuel. In a seemingly instantaneous burst, a wildfire overtakes thousands of acres of surrounding land, threatening the homes and lives of many in the vicinity.

An average of 5 million acres burn every year in the United States, causing millions of dollars in damage. Once a fire begins, it can spread at a rate of up to 14.29 miles per hour (23 kph), consuming everything in its path. As a fire spreads over brush and trees, it may take on a life of its own — finding ways to keep itself alive, even spawning smaller fires by throwing embers miles away.

After combustion occurs and a fire begins to burn, three factors control how the fire spreads. Depending on these factors, a fire can quickly fizzle out or turn into a raging blaze that scorches thousands of acres. These three factors are

- Fuel
- Weather
- Topography

Wildfires spread based on the type and quantity of fuel that surrounds them. Fuel can include everything from trees, underbrush, and dry grass to homes. The amount of flammable material that surrounds a fire is referred to as the fuel load. Fuel load is measured by the amount of available fuel per unit area, usually tons per acre. A small fuel load will cause a fire to burn and spread slowly, with a low intensity. If there is a lot of fuel, the fire will burn more intensely, causing it to spread faster. The faster it heats up the material around it, the faster those materials can ignite.

Because vegetation is the primary fuel for wildfires, the Federal Emergency Management Agency (FEMA) recommends a minimum 30-foot safety zone around your home. You should

- Limit the number and size of plants within this zone.
- Replace highly flammable species with less flammable vegetation.
- Limb trees from their base up to about 15 feet up the tree.
- Remove any climbing vines or espalier attached to your home.
- Cut grass and prune trees and shrubs in this area regularly.
- Remove plant debris such as broken limbs and fallen leaves.

A second zone, extending to 100 feet from the house, is also suggested. In this zone, you should lower the volume of vegetation and replace highly flammable trees and shrubbery with less flammable varieties.

Landscape foliage isn't the only culprit to be found around your home. You should also consider what your house is made of and any combustible items you store nearby. If you live in an area that has a history of wildfire activity, your home may already be outfitted with fire-retardant materials. For example, a slate or metal roof is much better than regular shingles. Check any outside storage closets or buildings for flammable items like paint, kerosene, gasoline, or propane and move these items 10 to 15 feet away from your home or any other structures. This includes moving that gas grill off your deck.

Temperature has a direct effect on the sparking of wildfires. Sticks, trees, and underbrush on the ground receive radiant heat from the sun, which heats and dries potential fuels. Warmer temperatures allow for fuels to ignite and burn faster, adding to the rate at which a wildfire spreads. For this reason, wildfires tend to rage in the afternoon, when temperatures are at their hottest.

Wind probably has the biggest impact on a wildfire's behavior. It is also the most unpredictable factor. Winds supply the fire with additional oxygen, provide even more dry potential fuel, and push the fire across the land at a faster rate.

The stronger the wind blows, the faster the fire spreads. The fire generates winds of its own that are as much as 10 times faster than the ambient wind. It can even throw embers into the air and create additional fires, called *spotting*. Wind can also change the direction of the fire, and gusts can raise the fire into the trees, creating a crown fire. Obviously, you can't do anything to change the weather, but you can be aware of it. If a wildfire is in your area, you will want to watch the weather and note any changes in wind direction or speed or humidity. When the humidity is low, meaning that there is a low amount of water vapor in the air, wildfires are more likely to start. The higher the humidity, the less likely the fuel is to dry and ignite.

Another big influence on wildfire behavior is the lay of the land, or *topography*. Although it remains virtually unchanged over time, unlike fuel and weather, topography can either aid or hinder wildfire progression. The most important factor in topography is slope. Unlike humans, fires usually travel uphill much faster than downhill. The steeper the slope, the faster the fire travels. Fires travel in the direction of the ambient wind, which usually flows uphill. Additionally, the fire is able to preheat the fuel farther up the hill because the smoke and heat are rising in that direction. Once the fire has reached the top of a hill, it must struggle to come back down because it's not able to preheat the downhill fuel. So, if you live on a hill you will want to follow the steps listed above, making sure that your zone covers the downhill side of your property. Furthermore, according to FEMA, you should extend the safety zone beyond the minimum 30 feet. Remember, the idea is to interrupt the fuel source so that the fire cannot spread.

Another thing you should do, whether you're in the vicinity of wildfire activity or not, is have an evacuation plan. In the event of a wildfire, this plan should not only include getting out of your house — make sure you have fire ladders for upper floors — but also an escape route with alternates just in case any roads are blocked off.

What if a main water supply gets infected with some form of bacteria?

One of the miracles of modern society is the abundant supply of clean drinking water available in every home and business. All you have to do is turn on the tap to drink clean, germ-free water. We take this miracle completely for granted, but if you ever travel to a country that doesn't have a good water system, you will quickly learn to appreciate the incredible convenience of our water system.

What would happen in the United States if a main water supply were to become contaminated by some sort of bacteria? Bacteria have a difficult time getting into drinking water because the water system is designed to keep them out. A typical water system pumps raw water from a river or a lake, removes the sediment in a settling tank, filters the water with a sand filter, and then decontaminates it with chlorine, ozone, and/or ultraviolet light to kill any bacteria that remain. The result is clear, healthy drinking water completely free of germs.

There are times, however, when the purification systems break down. This is especially common in small water systems in rural areas, where the water is not tested or monitored regularly. But it can also happen in big cities. The worst case so far happened in Milwaukee in 1993. A protozoa called cryptosporidium got into the water system, killing dozens of people and sickening approximately 400,000. The reason this protozoa was able to infect the water supply is that it's small, and therefore resistant to filtering, and because chlorine is not very effective against it. After the incident, Milwaukee installed an ozone system in addition to the chlorine system to guard against future occurrences.

In smaller water systems, especially those operating off of wells in rural areas, E. coli contamination of the well and poor monitoring can lead to problems. E. coli bacteria are killed by chlorine, but the concentration has to be high enough and the exposure time long enough for the chlorine to be effective. Certain strains of E. coli are deadly, especially to children and senior citizens.

So the answer to the question "What if the city water supply gets contaminated?" is "It could infect half the people in the city." The solution to this problem is constant and careful monitoring of the purification process, along with the use of several different purification systems to handle the different kinds of contamination.

What if I wanted to build a Great Pyramid today? How much would it cost?

Let's say that you want to create a theme park called *Egypt World,* complete with an authentic reconstruction of Egypt's Great Pyramid as the centerpiece for your park. What would you have to do, and would modern technology make the project any easier?

If you wanted to be completely authentic about it, you would do the whole project with people power. It's believed the Great Pyramid was built with the labor of 5,000, 20,000, or 100,000 people (depending on which expert is doing the estimate) over the course of 20 years or so. No matter how you slice it, that's a lot of man-years of effort. Even if you paid your workers minimum wage, just the labor for the project would cost billions of dollars.

The Great Pyramid is also amazing from a materials standpoint. The pyramid measures 756 by 756 feet at the base and is 481 feet tall. It is made up of more than 2 million blocks weighing on the order of 3 tons each. To build it out of blocks you would have to find a quarry containing that much stone, cut the stone out of the quarry, load it onto a truck or a train, haul it to the site, unload it, lift it, and so on. Working with stone blocks is definitely going to be a major pain. It's certainly doable, but it's a pain nonetheless.

There must be an easier way. Using today's technology, there is. To do it the modern way, you would definitely go with concrete. It would be something like building the Hoover Dam, which has about as much concrete in it as the Great Pyramid has stone. With concrete you can mold the shape you want and pour.

The Hoover Dam required over 3 million cubic yards of concrete. Because of the setting time for concrete and the amount of heat it generates during the setting process, the dam was poured in sections approximately 50 by 50 feet on a side and 5 feet deep. Workers embedded cooling pipes in the concrete as they poured it, and cold water ran through these pipes to help remove the heat during setting. A 5-foot-deep block would set for 36 to 72 hours before another block was poured on top of it. Using this tech- nique, the entire Hoover Dam was poured in less than 2 years.

This same technique would work great for re-creating the Great Pyramid. The Great Pyramid is even a little smaller than the Hoover Dam — only about 2.5 million cubic yards of concrete are needed. But this is still going to be an expensive project. If you're buying it by the truckload, concrete costs about $80 per square yard. For a big job like this, you would build your own concrete plant. Let's say that by doing so you get the cost down to $50 per square yard. That means concrete alone will cost $125 million. By the time you add in labor, design costs, form work, and so on, you probably end up doubling that. So your new Great Pyramid might cost something on the order of $250 million to $300 million.

What if we covered a city in a giant glass dome?

There is a very funny conversation that happens between Calvin and Hobbes in one of their comic strips. It goes like this:

> Hobbes: A new decade is coming up.
>
> Calvin: Yeah, big deal! Humph. Where are the flying cars? Where are the Moon colonies? Where are the personal robots and the zero gravity boots, huh? You call this a new decade?! You call this the future?? Ha! Where are the rocket packs? Where are the disintegration rays? Where are the floating cities?

Hobbes: Frankly, I'm not sure people have the brains to manage the technology they've got.

Calvin: I mean, look at this! We still have the weather?! Give me a break!

People think about domed cities because, as Calvin points out, we haven't figured out a way to control the weather. If everywhere in the world could have weather like San Diego, it probably would not be an issue. Unfortunately, in big cities like Buffalo, Minneapolis, New York, and Chicago, the weather is decidedly NOT San Diego–like, especially in the winter!

The goal of a domed city is to take a large urban area and cover it so that:

- The temperature is the same year round.
- There is never any rain or snow to spoil picnics and weddings.
- The cancerous effects of the sun are eliminated during outdoor activities.

There have been lots of attempts to create domed cities on a very small scale. Consider these examples:

- The Mall of America near Minneapolis is a tiny city under glass. It contains about 80 acres of floor space (on 27 acres of ground) holding more than 500 stores, 80 restaurants, and an indoor amusement park.
- Biosphere 2 is a giant, completely sealed lab covering 3.15 acres.
- The two Eden greenhouses in England are geodesic domes that together cover about 5 acres.
- Any domed stadium covers 8 to 10 acres.

What if we were to expand on these projects in a massive way, moving up to city-size and covering somewhere on the order of 650 acres — approximately a square mile? We're talking about taking a square parcel of land measuring approximately 1 mile on each side, or a circular piece of land measuring 1.13 miles in diameter, and completely covering it.

The first question is what technology would we use to cover such a huge space. Here are three possibilities:

- The Mall of America uses typical mall construction technologies — concrete and block walls, trusses, skylights, and so on. It's not very glamorous or inspiring architecture

Land and Sea

(there would be lots of supporting posts and walls in the city, rather than the dazzle of a mile-wide dome), but it is easy to imagine a construction process using these same techniques to cover a square mile.

- The Eden project uses a geodesic dome and hexagonal panels covered with multiple, inflatable layers of a very light plastic foil. The weight of the geodesic frame plus the hexagonal panels is about equal to the weight of the air contained inside the dome.

- The British Columbia Place Stadium is covered with a Teflon-coated fiberglass fabric held up by air pressure. The air pressure inside is only 0.03 psi higher than normal atmospheric pressure. Sixteen 100-horsepower fans provide the extra pressure.

In a project like covering a city with a dome, it may be that buildings form part of the structure for the dome. For example, six tall buildings at the center of the city could act as six pillars supporting the dome's center, with other buildings throughout the city acting as shorter pillars.

Certainly, using the mall technology, and probably using either of the other two technologies, it is easy to create a protective shell covering a square mile. Here are some of the more interesting questions that would be raised if someone actually tried to do this:

How many people could live there? We'll assume that the interior of the dome is developed at an average height of 10 stories. Some buildings will be higher, while some places in the city will be parks or otherwise undeveloped, working out to an average of 10 stories. That gives the city about 280,000,000 square feet of floor space. If you assume that the average person needs about 500 square feet of living space (pretty typical in suburban America), another 500 square feet of working space (for students it's classroom space, for white collar workers it's office space, and so on), and 500 square feet of open space for things like hallways, walkways, parks, common areas, elevators, and so on, then this city could house almost 200,000 people. However, it's likely that real estate under the dome will be extremely valuable and that people will fit into much smaller spaces than they typically do today. In other words, the space occupied per person might total only 500 square feet. That would allow the city to hold over half a million people.

How much would it cost to build? In today's dollars, space in a skyscraper costs something on the order of $400 per square foot to build. The Eden greenhouses cost something on the order of $400 per square foot too, so let's use that number. Let's estimate the cost of the dome per square foot of floor space that it covers at $100, for a total cost of $500 per square foot. The total cost for this project would be something on the order of $140 billion, or $250,000 per resident. That's not so unreasonable, when you think about it.

What will it cost to heat and cool this huge structure? That's impossible to say, because it depends on the type of construction, the location, and so on. However, it is interesting to note that the Mall of America doesn't have to spend money on heating, even though it's located in Minnesota. The lights and people provide plenty of heat. The problem will be cooling this massive structure, especially when the sun is shining. One way to solve this dilemma would be to locate the domed city in a very cold climate.

How will people get around? The maximum distance between any two points in the city will be about one mile, meaning that a person can walk anywhere in a half-hour or less. Walking will be the primary, and possibly the only, means of transportation for the residents of the city. There will need to be some way to accommodate the movement of food and retail products into the city. Underground train systems or roads for trucks might be the best solution.

The thing that you come to understand after thinking about a domed city is that it's not such a far-fetched idea. There's a good chance that we will see such a city developed over the next decade or two. Finally, people will be able to plan their weekends without having to worry about the weather!

What if the U.S. put all its trash in one giant landfill?

Right now in the United States there are landfills everywhere. However, it is getting harder and harder to create new landfills because no one wants to live near them. So, what if the U.S. were to create one gigantic landfill in a remote part of the country and start filling it with all of the municipal trash that America generates every day? How big would this landfill have to be?

Depending on which part of the country a person lives in and where the information is coming from, estimates are that an average person in the U.S. produces something like 3 to 4 pounds of trash per day. That trash comes from all sorts of things: used food containers (bottles, cans, pizza boxes), old newspapers and magazines, worn-out clothing, worn-down carpet, used-up batteries, broken appliances and toys, Styrofoam cups and packing material, junk mail, disposable diapers . . . you name it.

From a landfill perspective, it's not so much the weight of the trash as it is the volume of trash that matters. Things like Styrofoam, crumpled-up paper, and empty bottles and cans take up a lot of space for their weight. In other words, trash is very light for its volume, relatively speaking. Water weighs 1 gram per cubic centimeter. A trash bag full of trash easily floats on water. So let's pick an average density for trash of 0.33 grams per cubic centimeter.

Finally, let's assume that there arc 300 million people living in the United States.

This means that, in one year, 300 million people, each producing 3.5 pounds of trash per day, create something like 18,433,779,281 cubic feet of trash. Which is a lot. If you made the pile 400 feet deep (as tall as a 40-story building), it would cover over 1,000 acres of land.

If you keep filling up this landfill for 100 years, and if you assume that during this time the population of the United States doubles, then the landfill will cover about 160,000 acres, or 250 or so square miles, with trash 400 feet deep.

Here's another way to think about it. The Great Pyramid in Egypt is 756 by 756 feet at the base and is 481 feet tall, and anyone who has seen it in real life knows that it is a huge thing — one of the biggest things ever built by man. If you took all the trash that the United States would generate in 100 years and piled it up in the shape of the Great Pyramid, it would be about 32 times bigger. So the base of this trash pyramid would be about 4.5 miles by 4.5 miles, and the pyramid would rise almost 3 miles high.

That's a lot of trash!

What if there were no gravity on earth? What if gravity doubled?

Gravity is one of those things we take completely for granted. And there are two things about it that we take for granted: the fact that it is always there, and the fact that it never changes. If the earth's gravity were ever to change significantly, it would have a huge effect on nearly everything because so many things are designed around the current state of gravity.

Before looking at changes in gravity, however, it's helpful to first understand what gravity is. Gravity is an attractive force between any two atoms. Let's say you take two golf balls and place them on a table. There will be an incredibly slight gravitational attraction between the atoms in those two golf balls. If you use two massive pieces of lead and some amazingly precise instruments, you can actually measure an infinitesimal attraction between them. It is only when you get a gigantic number of atoms together, as in the case of the planet earth, that the force of gravitational attraction is significant.

The reason gravity on earth never changes is that the mass of the earth never changes. The only way to suddenly change the gravity on earth would be to change the mass of the planet. A change in mass great enough to result in a change in gravity isn't going to happen anytime soon.

But let's ignore the physics and imagine that one day the planet's gravity turned off, and suddenly there was no force of gravity on planet earth. This would turn out to be a pretty bad day. We depend on gravity to hold so many things down — cars, people, furniture, pencils and papers on your desk, and so on. Everything not stuck in place would suddenly have no reason to stay down, and it would start floating. But it's not just furniture and the like that would start to float. Two of the more important things held on the ground by gravity are the atmosphere and the water in our oceans, lakes, and rivers. Without gravity, the air in the atmosphere would have no reason to hang around, and it would immediately leap into space. This is the problem the moon has — the moon does not have enough gravity to keep an atmosphere

Land and Sea

33

around it, so it is in a near vacuum. Without an atmosphere, any living thing would die immediately, and anything liquid would boil away into space.

In other words, no one would last long if the planet didn't have gravity.

If gravity were to suddenly double, the result would be almost as bad, because everything would be twice as heavy. There would be big problems with anything structural. Houses, bridges, skyscrapers, table legs, support columns, and so on are all sized for normal gravity. Most structures would collapse fairly quickly if you doubled the load on them. Trees and plants would have problems. Power lines would have problems. The air pressure would double and that would have a big effect on the weather.

What this answer shows is just how integral gravity is to our world. We can't live without it, and we can't afford to have it change. It is one of the true constants in our lives!

3

On the Road

✿ What if I put sugar in a car's gas tank? • What if I put diesel fuel in an automobile that required unleaded fuel only? • What if I tried to drive my car underwater? • What if I threw my car into reverse while I was driving down the highway? • What if Formula One racetracks were loop-the-loop shaped instead of flat on the ground? • What if my brakes stopped working? • What if I never changed the oil in my car? • What if I pumped pure oxygen into my car engine instead of using the air in the atmosphere? • What if my car could run on ethanol — how much corn would I need to fuel a cross-country drive? • What if I put a 1 horsepower engine into my car?

What if I put sugar in a car's gas tank?

For some reason, there's a common rumor about sugar and gas that's been around for decades. Supposedly, if you pour sugar into someone's gas tank, you will disable the car. The sugar is supposed to react with the gasoline and turn into a semi-solid gooey substance that totally clogs up the gas tank, the fuel lines, and so on.

It sounds great, especially if you have a grudge against someone. The problem with this rumor is that it simply is not true. As it turns out, sugar doesn't dissolve in gasoline. Pouring sand into the gas tank would have about the same effect as pouring in sugar. The sand or sugar might clog up the filter, and that could disable the car, but it's not a sure thing.

So what do you do if you really want to disable someone's car? Pour in some water. Gasoline floats on top of water, so if you pour in several cups of water, the fuel pump will fill the fuel lines with water instead of gasoline and the car will have some major problems.

Another option, of course, is to drain all of the gasoline out of the tank. Or, if you can get the hood open, you could remove the battery — that totally disables the electrical system, including the spark plugs and the computer that controls the engine in most modern cars. Or you could light the car on fire. . . .

What if I put diesel fuel in an automobile that required unleaded fuel only?

Suppose you were to pull up to a gas station in a distracted state of mind. For example, you're driving your three children, plus three of their friends, to the zoo and they are all screaming for ice cream. As a result of this distraction, you accidentally reach for the diesel-fuel nozzle instead of the unleaded-gasoline nozzle and fill your tank. What would happen?

The first thing to recognize is that this scenario is not possible in most cars. In any car manufactured in the last 25 years or so, there's a plate under the gas cap that prevents anything but the small unleaded-gasoline nozzle from fitting into the tank. When unleaded gasoline first appeared, this plate helped to prevent drivers from putting the leaded-gasoline nozzle in — the unleaded and leaded nozzles were different sizes. The diesel nozzle is even bigger than leaded nozzles were, so it would never fit in the gas tank of most cars. However, most motorcycles and trucks don't have this plate, so it's easy to make this mistake if you're driving one of those vehicles. And if you're driving an older car, it won't have a plate either.

So say that you somehow filled a gasoline tank with diesel fuel. If you've ever compared gasoline to diesel fuel, you know that they smell different. They also feel different — diesel fuel is oily. Like oil, diesel fuel does not evaporate like gasoline does. Plus, diesel fuel is heavier. A gallon of diesel is about a pound heavier than a gallon of gasoline.

If you had a gas tank full of diesel fuel, the fuel injectors in your engine would inject the diesel fuel into the engine's cylinders. The spark plugs would fire, but nothing would happen after that. Because the diesel fuel doesn't evaporate very well, the spark plugs would have nothing to ignite, and the engine would never start.

To solve the problem, what you would do is drain all of the diesel fuel out of the gas tank and refill it with gasoline. Then you would have to keep cranking the engine for a while to get the diesel out of the fuel lines and the injectors. Eventually the engine would start and run fine. There would be no damage.

One obvious question from this discussion is: If diesel fuel won't burn in a gasoline engine, why does it burn in a diesel engine? There are two big differences between gas and diesel engines:

- First, diesel engines have no spark plugs.
- Second, they have much higher compression ratios. When the diesel engine compresses the air during its compression stroke, the air gets extremely hot. The diesel fuel is injected directly into this hot air, and it is hot enough to vaporize and ignite the diesel.

On the Road

❀

37

What if I tried to drive my car underwater?

In a lot of movies and military documentaries, you see Jeeps and military trucks nearly submerging themselves as they cross a river. These Jeeps and trucks can do it — what would happen if you tried to drive your submerged car through a shallow river or a 4-foot deep pond? Your car would die almost immediately. So what's the difference?

Creating a vehicle that can run submerged is a challenge. In order for any type of combustion engine to run, it must have a source of air and it must be able to release exhaust gasses. If the water isn't too deep (a few feet), the exhaust gases can take care of themselves because they come out with the engine under pressure.

The air intake is usually the problem. As soon as you submerge the air intake, the engine can no longer get air and it will stop running. You can get around the air intake problem by adding a snorkel to the air intake system. For example, military Humvees often have a snorkel attached to a port on the passenger side of the hood. The snorkel allows them to submerge in up to 5 feet (1.6 meters) of water and keep getting air.

Then you have to waterproof the engine. There are a lot of different issues to think about. For example:

- Any electrical devices, such as instruments, engine control computers, motors (for fans, windshield wipers, and so on), lights, and the battery, must be sealed.

- Any venting for items such as the crankcase and differential must be sealed (or vented at the same level as the snorkel).

- The fuel tank must be sealed and vented appropriately.

- Any chamber or crevice that can fill with water must have a drain.

If the air intake and exhaust have been taken care of and the engine has been completely waterproofed, then the vehicle can run underwater.

In general, waterproofing a diesel engine is easier than waterproofing a gasoline engine, because of the ignition system and sparkplugs in a gasoline engine. These components run at high voltage, and sealing them is very difficult (but not impossible). A diesel engine, on the other hand, has no ignition system. Also, if the diesel engine has a mechanical fuel pump for the injectors and a mechanical transmission, there are no engine control electronics to worry about. These features can make a diesel engine relatively easy to waterproof. That's why most military vehicles that ford rivers or run submerged have diesel engines.

What if I threw my car into reverse while I was driving down the highway?

This is one of those funny questions that pops up in lots of people's minds. As you're driving your car, you can imagine that it would be very easy to move the shifter into the "R" position at any time. You probably would never even consider giving in to your curiosity, though. Because you know that if you DID try it, you would cause the transmission to explode, or something like that. So instead, you end up constantly wondering. . . .

The reverse gear on any car with a manual transmission is an incredibly simple piece of machinery. There is a shaft that gets its power from the engine, and it has teeth on it that are used for reverse. There is another shaft that will drive the wheels, and it, too, has teeth on it that are used for reverse. To engage reverse, a gear literally gets pushed in between the two shafts to engage the two sets of teeth. It simply slides its teeth into the teeth on the two shafts and engages them. The image below shows this happening.

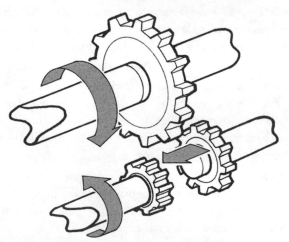

So it turns out that the answer to this question is pretty anticli-
mactic. If you were to actually try engaging reverse while rolling
down the road, the gear that has to slide into place is going to be
trying to engage two spinning gears, and one of those gears is
rotating rapidly in the wrong direction. What you will hear (and
feel in the shifter) is a very obnoxious buzzing sound as the teeth
gnash against one another. However, there is no way to get the
gear into place while in motion like this, so nothing will happen.
The transmission will not explode. Nor will the car stop on a
dime and reverse into oncoming traffic, even though that is what
happens in cartoons.

About the only time you can actually get a car into reverse is
when it is at a dead stop.

What if Formula One racetracks were loop-the-loop shaped instead of flat on the ground?

If you have ever looked at a Formula One car, an Indy car, or a
Champ car, you know that a big part of the car's body is the
aerodynamics package. At the front and back of the car are
wings. However, these wings are mounted upside down. Their
purpose isn't providing lift, like the wings of an airplane. Instead,
they are meant to force the car down onto the track to provide
better traction and a more stable ride. Once a car gets above
about 200 mph, the car is glued to the track by the aerodynamic
forces from the wings. At this speed, the car could travel upside
down on the ceiling of a tunnel if it wanted to.

What this means is that as long as the car is always moving
above 200 mph, you can make the track just about any shape you
want. For example, you could make the track circular and make
the walls completely vertical. You could also make it loop-the-
loop, or have the cars drive upside down. It doesn't really matter,
because the car will stick itself to the road.

As long as the shape of the track does not expose drivers to more
than 4Gs (but preferably no more than 3Gs) and there is enough
force on the tires to keep them stuck firmly to the ground, the
cars and drivers can handle most any shape.

What if my brakes stopped working?

Suppose you're driving down the freeway one day. As you're about to take the exit, you tap on the brakes — and don't slow down. No matter how hard you press, nothing happens. You have no brakes! What are you going to do???

When you press on the brake pedal in almost all cars today, you are pushing on a piston. That piston pushes on brake fluid in the master cylinder, pressurizing the brake fluid. It flows through thin pipes, called brake lines, to pistons at each wheel. Those pistons apply pressure to the brake pads, and they squeeze against a disk or a drum to stop the car. If you were to have a catastrophic loss of brake fluid or if someone were to cut your brake lines, nothing would happen when you hit the brake pedal.

The first thing to do if you ever find yourself in the "no brakes!" situation is to try pumping the brakes. If your brake lines have a small leak (instead of a cut), you may be able to pump enough fluid into the system to get things under control.

The next thing is to try the emergency brake — this is definitely an emergency! If someone cut your brake lines, he or she was probably smart enough to cut the cable for the emergency brake as well, so let's say that you find that the emergency brake is out of commission too.

Now you officially have a problem. The next thing to try is the transmission. You can downshift a gear at a time and use the engine for braking. Lots of people do this with their manual transmission as a matter of habit. It works just as well with an automatic transmission. Drop to a lower gear, wait for your speed to decrease, and then drop down another gear. If there is a grassy median, you can drive onto it to aid the process. The surface of the grass and the uneven ground will provide a little resistance to help slow the car.

If you are doing all this and it looks like you're going to run into something before you get the car stopped, then think strategically. Given a choice between running into something solid — for example, the massive concrete post of a bridge — and something that will give way — for example, a chain-link fence — choose the object that will give way. If you can scrub off speed by edging the side of the car against a wall or a guardrail, that's a good idea. If you can drive up a rising embankment, that will also help.

In other words, if you have time to save the car by using something nondestructive like the transmission or an embankment, use it. If you can't save the car, then save yourself. Do whatever you can to avoid injury to yourself by running into something "soft" or scrubbing off the speed. And if that fails, then relax and hope your airbag is in good shape!

What if I never changed the oil in my car?

The blood in your body. Water in the desert. And oil in an engine. They are all vital. Without them, someone or something is going to die!

Oil is an essential lubricant in your engine. It lets metal press against metal without damage. For example, it lubricates the pistons as they move up and down in the cylinders. Without oil, the metal-on-metal friction creates so much heat that eventually the surfaces weld themselves together and the engine seizes. Which is not good if you are trying to get somewhere. On the other hand, if you want someone else NOT to get somewhere, then draining the oil out of his or her engine is an effective roadblock!

Let's say that your engine has plenty of oil, but you never change it. Two things will definitely happen:

- Dirt will accumulate in the oil. The filter will remove the dirt for a while, but eventually the filter will clog and the dirty oil will automatically bypass the filter through a relief valve. Dirty oil is thick and abrasive, so it causes more wear.

- Additives in the oil, like detergents, dispersants, rust fighters, and friction reducers will wear out, so the oil won't work as well as it should.

What will happen eventually, as the oil gets dirtier and dirtier, is that the oil will stop lubricating and the engine will quickly wear and fail. Don't worry, this is not going to happen if you forget to change your oil one month and it goes over the recommended change interval by 500 miles. You would have to run the same oil through the engine for a long time — many thousands of miles — before it caused catastrophic failure.

The three good things you get from an oil change are a clean filter, clean oil, and fresh oil additives, so the oil provides peak lubrication.

What if I pumped pure oxygen into my car engine instead of using the air in the atmosphere?

The internal combustion engine in most cars burns gasoline. To do the burning an engine needs oxygen, and the oxygen comes from the air all around us. But what if cars carried their own oxygen and pumped pure oxygen into the engine instead?

Air is about 21% oxygen. Almost all the rest is nitrogen, which is inert when it runs through the engine. The oxygen controls how much gasoline an engine can burn. The ratio of gas to oxygen is about 1:14 — for each gram of gasoline that burns, the engine needs about 14 grams of oxygen. The engine can burn no more gas than the amount of oxygen allows. Any extra fuel would come out the exhaust pipe unburned.

So if the car used pure oxygen, it would be inhaling 100% oxygen instead of 21% oxygen, or about five times more oxygen. This would mean that it could burn about five times more fuel. And that would mean about five times more horsepower. So a 100 horsepower engine would become a 500 horsepower engine!

So why don't cars carry around pure oxygen? The problem is that oxygen is pretty bulky, even when you compress it, and an engine uses a LOT of oxygen. A gallon of gasoline weighs 6.2 pounds, so the engine needs 86.8 pounds of oxygen (6.2 × 14) per gallon of gasoline. Oxygen is a gas, so it is extremely light. One pound of oxygen fills 11.2 cubic feet of space, so a gallon of gasoline needs 972.16 cubic feet of oxygen to go with it. If your gas tank holds 20 gallons of gasoline, you would have to carry almost 20,000 cubic feet of oxygen with it! This is a lot of oxygen — so much that it would fill a 2,500 square foot house.

Even if you compress the oxygen to 3,000 psi (pounds per square inch), it will still take 100 cubic feet to store it. To put that into perspective, a standard scuba tank only holds about 0.4 cubic feet of compressed gas — that's about 80 cubic feet of uncompressed gas, so it would take 250 scuba tanks to hold all that oxygen.

Because oxygen is so bulky, what people use instead is nitrous oxide. In the engine, nitrous oxide turns into nitrogen and oxygen, and it's the oxygen that people are after. Nitrous oxide easily liquefies under pressure, so you can store a lot more of it in a bottle than you can gaseous oxygen, which does not liquefy. Even so, a typical system will only supply 1 to 3 minutes of nitrous to the engine. In the process, it adds about 100 horsepower to a typical big block engine. The biggest problem is that the extra gasoline that the nitrous oxide allows in the cylinder increases pressure in the engine so much that it can do some real damage, unless the engine is designed to handle it. That would be the same problem you would have with an engine breathing pure oxygen — it would have to be quite beefy to handle the load.

What if my car could run on ethanol — how much corn would I need to fuel a cross-country drive?

Ethanol, or ethyl alcohol, is made by fermenting and distilling simple sugars from corn. Ethanol is sometimes blended with gasoline to produce gasohol. Ethanol-blended fuels account for 12% of all automotive fuels sold in the United States, according to the Renewable Fuels Association. In very pure forms, ethanol can be used as an alternative to gasoline in vehicles that have been modified for its use. In order to calculate how much corn you would have to grow to produce enough ethanol to fuel a trip across the country, there are a couple of basic factors to consider:

- Let's assume that you drive a Toyota Camry, the best-selling car in America in 2000. We know that the Toyota Camry with automatic transmission gets 30 miles per gallon of gas on the highway.

- Ethanol is less efficient than gasoline. One gallon of gasoline is equal to 1.5 gallons of ethanol. This means that same Camry would only get about 20 miles to the gallon when it's running on ethanol.

- Let's say you're traveling from Los Angeles to New York, which is roughly 2,774 miles (4,464 km).

With these numbers, you can figure out how much fuel you will need:

2,774 miles ÷ 20 miles per gallon = 138.7 gallons

(Metric: 4,464 km ÷ 8.5 km per liter = 525.2 liters)

Through research performed at Cornell University, we know that one acre of land can yield about 7,110 pounds (3,225 kg) of corn. That corn can be processed into 328 gallons (1,240 liters) of ethanol. That's about 26.1 pounds (11.84 kg) of corn per gallon.

With this information, you can calculate how many pounds of corn you need to fuel the Camry on its trip:

138.7 gallons × 26.1 pounds = 3,620.07 total pounds of corn

(Metric: 525.2 liters × 3.13 kg = 1,642 kg)

You will need to plant a little more than a half an acre of corn to produce enough ethanol to fuel your trip.

What if I put a 1 horsepower engine into my car? Wouldn't I save a lot of money on gasoline?

A typical car in America has something around a 120 horsepower engine. A big SUV might have a 200 horsepower engine, and a tiny car might have only 70 horsepower. A moped, on the other hand, has only a 1 or 2 horsepower engine, and it gets great gas mileage — 70 or 80 miles per gallon. So why not put a little engine in a car to give its mileage a boost?

One reason is that a car needs a fair amount of power to make its way down the road. At 60 mph, a typical car needs 10 to 20 horsepower simply to maintain its speed. That energy level is needed to overcome wind resistance and the rolling resistance in the tires. If you have the headlights on, the alternator is using power to generate electricity for the lights. If the air conditioner is on, that takes power too. A 1 horsepower engine could not maintain more than 20 or 30 miles per hour in a normal car, and you could never turn on the headlights or the air conditioning.

The other problem is acceleration. Your car has a 120 horsepower engine — even though all you need is 10 or 20 horsepower to go down the road — for those moments when you want to accelerate up to a high speed very quickly. The bigger the engine, the faster you can accelerate. With a 1 horsepower engine, you might need a couple of minutes to accelerate up to 60 mph, even if there were no such thing as wind resistance.

If you wanted to make a car that could run on a 1 horsepower engine, you would need to make it a tiny, lightweight, extremely aerodynamic one-seater. It would look more like a cold capsule than a car. By making it tiny and lightweight, you would be able to accelerate quickly even with limited power. Because it would be minuscule and aerodynamic, you would reduce its wind resistance so much that a 1 horsepower engine could keep it moving at 60 or 70 mph without any trouble. That would give you a super-high-mileage car.

4

Body and Mind

✺ What if people had exoskeletons? • What if I never cut my hair? Would I look like Cousin It from *The Addam's Family?* • What if I never took a bath? • What if I were struck by lightning? • What if we didn't have eyebrows? • What if I couldn't burp or get rid of gas any other way — would I explode? • What if I stopped sleeping — never slept again, ever? • What if I only consumed peanut butter every day for the rest of my life? • What if I got bonked really hard on my head? Would I lose my memory? • What if I were to breathe 100% oxygen?

What if people had exoskeletons?

Human beings are like reptiles, amphibians, birds, and fish in that we all have internal skeletons. Muscles connect to the skeleton to provide motion, and we have soft skin on the outside. A huge percentage of the life on this planet does it the other way around. Many animals have their skeletons on the outside, in the form of exoskeletons. Insects are the most common example, and then there are crustaceans like lobsters.

Why might humans want to have exoskeletons? Anyone who has ever tried to crack open a crab leg knows that exoskeletons are strong. An exoskeleton would certainly cut down on cuts and bruises, and it would also eliminate the need for all those pads that professional football players have to wear!

So why don't people have exoskeletons? The biggest reason we don't have exoskeletons is that, physiologically speaking, it is highly impractical and could actually be pretty dangerous. Many creatures that have exoskeletons experience a process known as *molting* — they lose their entire outside shell and replace it with a new one. Unfortunately, the new exoskeleton is not completely intact or finished when the previous one is shed. The time it takes the new encasement to harden is directly related to the size of the creature. The larger the animal, the longer it takes. During this time, the animal is extremely vulnerable, exposed to the elements, predators, and even disease.

Although having real exoskeletons wouldn't be prudent for humans, some folks believe there are reasons for fashioning a wearable variety. Humans aren't the swiftest creatures on earth, and we're limited in the amount of weight that we can pick up and carry. These weaknesses can be fatal on the battlefield, and that's why the U.S. Defense Advanced Research Projects Agency (DARPA) is investing $50 million to develop an exoskeleton suit for ground troops. This wearable robotic system could give soldiers the ability to run faster, carry heavier weapons, and leap over large obstacles. These exoskeletal machines could be equipped with sensors and global positioning system (GPS) receivers. Soldiers could use this technology to obtain information about the terrain they are crossing and how to navigate their way to specific locations. DARPA is also developing computerized fabrics that could be used with the exoskeletons to monitor heart and breathing rates.

Basically, these wearable machines would give humans enhanced abilities. Imagine a battalion of super soldiers who can lift hundreds of pounds as easily as lifting 10 pounds and who can run twice their normal speed. The potential for non-military applications is also phenomenal.

If the U.S. military has its way, it will have throngs of super soldiers who can jump higher, run faster, and lift enormous weight by strapping these exoskeletons on themselves. However, developing these devices is expected to take years, if not decades.

What if I never cut my hair? Would I look like Cousin It from *The Addam's Family*?

Typical human hair consists of the hair shaft, which sticks through the skin, and the root, which is sunk in a follicle, or pit, beneath the skin's surface. Except for a few growing cells at the base of the root, the hair is dead tissue made up of keratin and related proteins. The hair follicle is a tube-like pocket of the epidermis that encloses a small section of the dermis at its base. Cells divide rapidly at the base of the follicle to form human hair. As the cells push upward from the follicle's base, they harden and undergo pigmentation. And, voilà, you have hair.

Okay, so this process happens over and over again. You're probably thinking that if you never cut your hair, it would just grow and grow and who knows how long it would be. It's not that simple. Your hair actually doesn't just grow and grow. At any given time, some of your roots (about 15% or so) are actually on a growth hiatus. For about three months there is no activity in those follicles. Which means no hair growth at that particular site on your scalp. You also lose hair every day, either due to normal shedding or damage. On average, you lose anywhere from 50 to 100 hairs every day.

The hairs on our heads grow about half an inch per month, and have an average life of 2 to 6 years. From this, you can figure that an average person's hair should grow no longer than 3 feet or so.

.5 inches × 12 months × 6 years = 36 inches, or 3 feet

Considering some peoples' hair might grow a little faster and could possibly remain attached to their head for a longer period of time, it's possible that a person's hair might grow even longer than that, say about 5 feet. But that would certainly be less common. So, it's highly unlikely that you would resemble Cousin It from *The Addam's Family*.

It is interesting to note, however, that there have been documented cases in the Guinness Book of World Records citing considerably longer heads of hair. In 1993, Dian Witt of Massachusetts reportedly had locks measuring 12 feet 8 inches in length, and in 1994, Mata Jagdamba of India sported tresses 13 feet 10½ inches long.

What if I never took a bath?

Your initial thought as you ponder this question might involve the word "gross." Beyond the immediate ramifications involving odors and a marked decline in social invitations from friends and family members are concerns of a more serious nature — the health variety.

Think about what's going to happen if you decide to stop bathing:

- You will smell bad.
- Your skin and hair gets dirtier and dirtier.
- Your chance of infection goes up.
- You will probably itch a lot more, and this could lead to an even higher risk of infection.

Consider what is going to get and remain dirty if you never bathe. The average human body is covered by about 20 square feet (2 square meters) of skin containing about 2.6 million sweat glands. In addition to sweat glands, your skin houses thousands of tiny hairs.

You are constantly sweating, even though you may not notice it. There are two kinds of sweat glands all over your body — eccrine and apocrine. The sweat from apocrine glands contains proteins and fatty acids, which make it thick and give it a milky or yellowish color. This is why underarm stains in clothing appear yellowish. It turns out that sweat itself has no odor. Then why, you may ask, is a sweaty person so smelly? When the bacteria on your skin and hair metabolize the proteins and fatty acids, they produce an unpleasant odor.

An average person can sweat something like 1 to 3 liters per hour depending on the surrounding climate. Let's say you're sweating as much as 3 liters every hour. Because your skin, along with the hair all over your body, is sticky with sweat, it's probably picking up even more grunge than usual. We're just talking surface grime here — regular old dirt. What about the other germs and microorganisms your skin regularly plays host to? For the most part, these bacteria, fungi, and yeasts prove no major threat — as long as they remain on the skin's surface. However, if they reach the bloodstream, that can be quite a different story.

There are a number of things that can make a person itch. Anyone can get chiggers or ringworm. Normally, this isn't such a big deal. Get some medicated ointment, and you will be fine. But if you are on a bathing hiatus and you're already quite itchy, either one of these conditions could send you into a scratching frenzy. You might scratch so much that you break your skin's surface. Now, let's say you have some serious bacteria hanging around in all that grime — perhaps staphylococcus. If it were to enter your bloodstream through the open scratches, the situation could even become fatal. The chances of this happening, though, are probably fairly small.

All of that aside, it's highly likely that the stink factor is enough to send you scurrying for the soapsuds on a regular basis.

What if I was struck by lightning?

Initially, this seems like a fairly straightforward question. As it turns out, there are several ways a person can be struck by lightning, and the type of strike dictates the impact it can have on your body:

- Direct strike — a cloud-to-ground lightning strike hits you or something you're holding, like a golf club, dead on instead of reaching the ground.

- Side flash — lightning strikes something close to where you are standing and then jumps from that to you.

- Contact potential — while you are touching something, like a fencepost or a tree, lightning strikes that object and the current travels from the object through the point of contact into your body.

- Step voltage — you are sitting with your feet together in front of you, knees up, and rump settled on the ground near a spot where a cloud-to-ground lightning strike hits. As the lightning current disperses, it travels through your body by entering one point, say your joined feet, and exiting another, your rear end.

- Surge voltage — while you are using some type of electrical appliance or a telephone, lightning strikes the source of power or network connected to the device and you receive a shock.

The worst kind of lightning experience is a direct strike — statistically, it is the most fatal. Being hit by a side flash or through contact potential are the next in the level of severity, with step voltage third and surge voltage last. Basically, the amount of current and voltage going through your body lessens with each of these types of strikes. If you are a victim of a direct strike, the full impact of the lightning courses through your body. In the other scenarios, the intensity is lessened because some of the energy is dispersed elsewhere.

The circulatory, respiratory, and nervous systems are most commonly affected when a person is struck by lightning:

- **Circulatory:** Reportedly, the majority of fatalities resulting from direct strikes are due to cardiac arrest. Ironically, were someone nearby with an automatic external defibrillator to administer another electric shock to the heart, the victim might survive.

- **Respiratory:** The greatest threat to the respiratory system is paralysis. Artificial respiration is required so the victim won't die from lack of oxygen.

- **Nervous:** When the central nervous system is affected, a number of side effects can occur, such as dementia, amnesia, temporary paralysis, impaired reflexes, memory gaps, and anxiety or depression.

Over 1,000 people get struck by lightning every year in the U.S., and over 100 of them die as a result of the strike. Lightning is not something to toy with. There are several precautions you can take to guarantee your safety in a storm.

If you are outside:

- Always look for appropriate shelter in a building or a car. Most people think it is the rubber tires that keep you safe in a car, because rubber does not conduct electricity. Actually, in strong electric fields, rubber tires become more conductive than insulating. The reason you are safe in a car is that the lightning will travel around the surface of the vehicle and then go to ground. The vehicle acts like a Faraday cage. Michael Faraday, a British physicist, discovered that a metal cage would shield objects within the cage when a high potential discharge hit the cage. The metal, being a good conductor, would direct the current around the objects and discharge the current safely to the ground. This process of shielding is widely used today to protect electrostatic sensitive integrated circuits in the electronics world.

- Avoid taking shelter under trees. Trees attract lightning. Instead, go to an open area and put your feet as close together as possible and crouch down with your head as low as possible without touching the ground — remember step voltage — you only want one contact point with the ground. Never lay down on the ground for the same reason; you never want the current to have the ability to pass through your body.

If you are inside:

- Stay off the phone. If you must call someone, use a cordless phone or cell phone. If lightning strikes the phone line, the strike will travel to every phone on the line and potentially to you, if you are holding the phone.

- Stay away from plumbing pipes (bath tub, shower). Lightning has the ability to strike a house or near a house and impart an electrical charge to the metal pipes used for plumbing. This threat is not as great as it used to be, because PVC (polyvinyl chloride) is often used for indoor plumbing these days. If you are not sure what your pipes are made of, wait it out.

What if we didn't have eyebrows?

In order to answer this question, we need to know what eyebrows do and why people have them.

Eyebrows are a very significant aspect of a person's appearance. They are one of the most distinctive features that make up a face, and many people pay a lot of attention to them. People think of some types of eyebrows as attractive and some as unattractive, and many people spend as much time preening their eyebrows as they do applying makeup to their eyelashes or lips. Eyebrows are also one of the most expressive facial features. One of the clearest ways to tell somebody what you're thinking is simply to move your eyebrows up or down — most everyone knows what different eyebrow positions mean.

Eyebrows obviously serve a lot of functions in our culture today — beauty, nonverbal communication, distinctive appearance. But why are they there in the first place? As humans evolved and lost most of the thick hair on their bodies, why did they keep that little bit over the eyes?

Scientists aren't entirely sure why this hair remains, but they have a pretty good guess. Eyebrows help keep moisture out of your eyes when you sweat or walk around in the rain. The arch shape diverts the flow of rain or sweat to the sides of your face, keeping your eyes relatively dry. The most obvious advantage, then, is that eyebrows let you see clearly when you're sweating a lot or are out in the rain. Without eyebrows, getting around in these conditions is a little more difficult. The shape of your brow itself diverts a certain amount of moisture, but eyebrows make a significant difference in your ability to see. Diverting the sweat away is also good because the salt in sweat irritates the eyes, making them sting a little.

There are a number of ways these qualities might have helped early humans survive. Being able to see more clearly in the rain could certainly help you find shelter, and there are several circumstances when keeping the sweat out of your eyes could save your life. If you were trying to outrun a predator, for example, it's a good bet that a lot of sweat would be running down your face. If all that sweat flowed right down into your eyes, you wouldn't be able to see that well, and your eyes would be irritated, which would certainly slow you down! Because of this slight survival advantage, nature would most likely select for humans with eyebrows over humans without eyebrows. Think about it this way — if you didn't have eyebrows, you might not even be here to ponder this question.

Most scientists are inclined to believe that if we didn't have eyebrows, something else would have evolved to help the situation. For example, humans could have developed incredibly thick eyelashes to shield out excess sweat or rain. Or, our skulls could have continued to protrude so that they formed a ledge above our eyes — rain or sweat would then drop from that ledge away from our faces, without going in our eyes.

What if I couldn't burp or get rid of gas any other way — would I explode?

This is a question that has certainly crossed the minds of children everywhere, and admittedly the minds of adults as well. To answer this question, first we need to look at how and why we expel gas in the first place. Humans rid themselves of excess gas in two ways — belching and flatulence.

Basically, what happens when you belch or burp is that air is being forced from your stomach up through your throat and out of your mouth. Sometimes this happens so quickly, there's hardly any time to politely cover your mouth. An apologetic "Excuse me" must suffice. Most often, eating or drinking something too quickly causes these unwanted bursts because, in addition to your food or beverage, you take in extra, unnecessary air with each gulp. Other culprits include carbonated beverages and drinking through a straw.

Flatulence is a little different. In this case, the gas is being voided from either your stomach or your intestines and it is leaving your body by way of the opposite end of your digestive tract. Most of us think that *flatus* (gas) is caused by specific foods. This is only part of the story. It is true that foods such as beans or dairy products can cause your body to produce extra gas. However, your body actually produces a certain amount of gas on a daily basis anyway — no matter if you have beans for lunch or forget to take a lactose pill before having a milkshake. Usually, the walls of your intestines absorb this gas. When there is too much gas for your bowels to absorb, your body finds another way to relieve the unwanted pressure.

So, what happens when you have too much gas for your intestines to absorb and you aren't able to break wind? It's not a pretty picture. You would actually be in a lot of pain. Initially you would feel bloated. Think about the way you feel after eating too much food or drinking too much water all at once. When you eat an excessive amount of food, things usually settle down after a bit. Unfortunately, that relief would not be forthcoming. Your stomach and intestines would most likely fill up with gas, much like a balloon with air. While you wouldn't explode exactly, that's pretty much what a good portion of your insides would do. The walls of your guts would stretch to their capacity, and would eventually perforate or rupture altogether.

What if I stopped sleeping — never slept again, ever?

In order to answer this, we need to look at some basics about sleep. The amount you need decreases with age. A newborn baby might sleep 20 hours a day. By age 4, the average is 12 hours a day. By age 10, the average falls to 10 hours a day. Most adults seem to need 7 to 9 hours of sleep a night. And senior citizens can often get by with 6 or 7 hours a day. These are just averages, and vary by person. You, for example, probably know how much sleep you need in an average night to feel your best.

You know you feel great after a good night of sleep. But, why is that? Does anything important happen during sleep? Yes, two things are known to happen during sleep. Growth hormone in children is secreted during sleep, and chemicals important to the immune system are secreted during sleep. You can become more prone to disease if you don't get enough sleep, and a child's growth can be stunted by sleep deprivation.

No one really knows why it is that we sleep, but there are all kinds of theories, including these:

- Sleep gives the body a chance to repair muscles and other tissues, replace aging or dead cells, and so on.

- Sleep gives the brain a chance to organize and archive memories. Dreams are thought by some to be part of the process.

- Sleep lowers our energy consumption, so we need three meals a day rather than four or five. Since we can't do anything in the dark anyway, we might as well "turn off" and save the energy.

- Sleep may be a way of recharging the brain.

A good way to understand why you sleep is to look at what happens when we don't get enough:

- As you know if you have ever pulled an all-nighter, missing one night of sleep is not fatal. A person will generally be irritable during the next day and will either slow down (become tired easily) or will be totally wired because of adrenalin.

- If a person misses two nights of sleep, it gets worse. Concentrating is difficult and attention span falls by the wayside. Mistakes increase.

- After three days, a person will start to hallucinate, and clear thinking is impossible. With continued wakefulness, a person can lose grasp on reality.

A person who gets just a few hours of sleep per night can experience many of the same problems over time.

It only takes three days of sleep deprivation to cause a person to hallucinate. Obviously, if you were to go for a longer period of time, the symptoms would worsen and, in time, would most likely prove fatal. Rats forced to stay awake continuously will eventually die, proving that sleep is definitely essential. So, unless you were being forced to stay awake, you'd probably fall asleep before something as drastic as death could happen.

It's interesting to know that some people can function on very little sleep if necessary. A portion of a Navy SEAL's rigorous training program is a good example of this phenomenon. During what is commonly called "Hell Week," the trainees must engage in highly physical activities for about six days — all of their hard work is accomplished on about 4 hours of sleep for the entire week!

What if I only consumed peanut butter every day for the rest of my life?

While peanut butter does offer quite a lot nutritionally, eating only one thing is never really a good idea. You first need to understand how food works, in general, to see why it is that man cannot survive by bread alone . . . or in this case, peanut butter.

Your body uses food to stay alive. Consider what you might have eaten today: a bagel, milk, juice, ham, cheese, an apple, french fries, and so on. All of these foods contain seven basic components. Each of these components operates in its own special way to keep your body working:

- **Carbohydrates (both simple and complex).** Carbohydrates and complex carbohydrates provide your body with its basic fuel. Your body uses carbohydrates like a car engine uses gasoline. Glucose, the simplest carbohydrate, flows in the bloodstream so that it is available to every cell in your body. Your cells absorb glucose and convert it into energy that drives the cells.

- **Proteins.** A protein is any chain of amino acids. An amino acid is a small molecule that acts as the building block of any cell. Carbohydrates provide cells with energy, while amino acids provide cells with the building material they need to grow and maintain their structure.

- **Vitamins.** Vitamins are smallish molecules that your body needs to keep itself running properly. The body can produce its own vitamin D, but generally vitamins must be provided by food. The human body needs 13 different vitamins. A diet of fresh, natural food usually provides all of the vitamins that you need. Processing tends to destroy vitamins; so many processed foods are "fortified" with man-made vitamins.

- **Minerals.** Minerals are elements that our bodies must have in order to create specific molecules needed in the body. Food provides these minerals. If they are lacking in the diet, then various problems and diseases can arise. Calcium is the most obvious mineral — your body uses it to build bones.

- **Fats.** Although you hear a lot about why you shouldn't have fat, you actually *need* to eat fat. Certain vitamins are fat-soluble (vitamins A, D, E, and K are all fat-soluble). The only way to get these vitamins is to eat fat. Another reason you need to eat fat: In the same way that there are essential amino acids, there are essential fatty acids (for example, linoleic acid is used to build cell membranes). You must obtain these fatty acids from food you eat because your body has no way to make them.

Fat also is a good source of energy. Fat contains twice as many calories per gram as carbohydrates or proteins. Your body can burn fat as fuel when necessary.

- **Fiber.** When you eat fiber, it simply passes straight through, untouched by the digestive system. But it is an important part of good nutrition just the same. Fiber intake has been positively linked to cholesterol reduction, better bowel function, and even a reduction in the risk of certain cancers.

- **Water.** Your body is about 70% water. A person at rest loses about 40 ounces of water per day. Water leaves your body in urine, in your breath when you exhale, by evaporation through your skin, and so on. Because you are losing water all the time, you must replace it. Obviously you need to take in at least 40 ounces a day in the form of moist foods and liquids. In hot weather and when exercising, your body may need twice that amount.

Okay, so now you know what the building blocks are for good nutrition. Let's look at how much of everything you need for your body to work properly.

The DRV (Daily Reference Value) recommended for protein is about 50 grams. If you wanted to get your daily requirement of protein, you'd have to eat between 12 and 14 tablespoons of peanut butter. If you were eating only peanut butter, though, you'd be eating more than that. You'd have to eat about 21 tablespoons of peanut butter to reach 2,000 calories a day (which is the least amount of calories you'd want to consume in a day, unless you're on a diet). You can see that if you only ate peanut butter, you would be consuming almost twice the recommended DRV of protein. So, you're getting (more than) enough protein — but what about the other stuff your body needs?

You know that peanut butter makes you thirsty, so let's assume you are supplementing your singular diet with 8 to 10 glasses of water a day, so that you don't become dehydrated. Protein — check;

water — check. But what else are you getting from the peanut butter? What about fiber, vitamins, carbohydrates, minerals, and fats?

As it turns out, your diet of peanut butter would supply 21 grams of fiber — very close to the DRV of 25 grams. It would also provide enough vitamin E and more than twice the RDI (Reference Daily Intake) of vitamin B3 (niacin), but you would be receiving less than one third the RDI for vitamins B1 and B2 (thiamin and riboflavin). Furthermore, supplementing your diet with the required RDI of vitamins A, C, D, and K would be necessary. Night blindness, scurvy, rickets, and poor blood clotting or internal bleeding have been associated with deficiencies of these vitamins, respectively. You would not be getting enough carbohydrates, either. The DRV of carbohydrates for a 2,000-calorie diet is 300 grams. The peanut butter would only supply 88 grams — less than a third of the recommended amount.

While your intake of copper and magnesium would be in line with the DRV, you would not be getting enough calcium, iron, or potassium. Okay, so you might be thinking that you'll simply take a multivitamin — problems solved. Not really — take a look at fat.

The DRV for fat is 65 grams for a 2,000-calorie-a-day diet. There are 168 grams of fat in 21 tablespoons of peanut butter. So that's more than two and a half times the DRV. Yikes! While a certain amount of fat is necessary for a well-balanced diet, a number of serious conditions, such as heart disease and certain cancers, have been linked to overconsumption of fat. Given that, you can see that a peanut butter–only diet is not ideal.

What if I got bonked really hard on my head? Would I lose my memory? Could I regain my memory by repeating the blow to my head?

Television shows that include this kind of memory loss are incorporating a condition called *amnesia* into their plot. Sometimes amnesia wipes out everything from a person's past, and other times just bits and pieces are missing.

It turns out that there are several types of amnesia, and they can be caused by things like disease, psychological trauma, and yes, even physical trauma such as a *severe* blow to the head. In most cases, amnesia is a temporary condition and is very brief, lasting from a few seconds to a few hours. However, the duration can be longer, depending on the severity of the disease or trauma, possibly lasting a few weeks or even months. The two types of amnesia you hear about most often are

- Retrograde amnesia
- Anterograde amnesia

Retrograde amnesia is basically a condition in which people can't recall stored memories, like their mom's maiden name or what happened last Christmas, but they may recall the knock-knock joke their little brother told them a few seconds ago. This is the kind of amnesia you see a lot on soap operas. A married couple is on their honeymoon cruise and somehow the bride falls overboard. After she's rescued, she has no memory of her life before the accident. She doesn't remember her husband or even that she's married, but she does remember the handsome crew member who plucked her from the ocean. Although you see this a lot on television, it doesn't happen that often in real life.

If someone has anterograde amnesia, he or she cannot remember incidents that happen after the onset of amnesia. A less common device in television or movie scripts, this form of amnesia is central to the plot of the movie *Memento*. The main character receives a severe blow to the head and suffers brain damage. Similar to other victims of anterograde amnesia, he can no longer form new memories.

As an amnesiac recovers, he or she usually recalls older memories first, and then more recent memories, until almost all memory is recovered. Memories of events that occurred around the time of the head trauma or onset of amnesia are sometimes never recovered.

When people talk about memory, they are usually thinking about what is known as long-term memory. People actually have several different forms of memory. The three most important types to consider when thinking about amnesia are

- **Short-term memory** — this refers to memories that last anywhere from a few seconds to a couple of minutes.
- **Intermediate long-term memory** — this refers to memories that may last for days or even weeks, but which eventually are lost forever unless they are moved to long-term memory.
- **Long-term memory** — this refers to memories that can be recalled for many years or perhaps for an entire lifetime.

In order to understand how the loss of memory works, knowing how we store memories in the first place is helpful. The human brain is a truly amazing organ. It gives us the power to think, plan, speak, and imagine. It also gives us the ability to make and store memories. Physiologically speaking, a memory is the result of chemical or even structural changes in synaptic transmissions between neurons. As these changes occur, a pathway is created. This pathway is called a memory trace. Signals can travel along these memory traces through the brain.

Making and storing memories is a complex process. It involves many regions of the brain, including the frontal, temporal, and parietal lobes. Damage or disease in these areas can result in varying degrees of memory loss.

Here's a good example of how memory loss can occur. For short-term memory to become long-term memory, it must go through a process known as consolidation. During consolidation, short-term memory is repeatedly activated — so much so that certain chemical and physical changes occur in the brain, permanently embedding the memory for long-term access. If, during this repeated activation, something interrupts the process — let's say a concussion or other brain trauma — then short-term memory cannot be consolidated. Memories can't be stored for long-term access. This may be what is going on in anterograde amnesia.

It is believed that consolidation takes place in the hippocampi, parts of the brain which are located in the temporal-lobe region of the brain. Medical research indicates that it is the frontal and temporal lobes that are most often damaged during head injury. This is why many people who suffer severe head trauma or brain injury experience anterograde amnesia. If the hippocampi are damaged, the amnesiac will be able to recall older memories, but won't be able to make any new ones.

So, yes, it is possible to suffer memory loss — amnesia — as the result of a blow to the head. But, the head trauma must be severe.

For a bonk on the head to result in amnesia, the bonk would have to be so incredibly hard that it would cause severe swelling around the temporal lobe and/or injury to this region of the brain. Obviously, another blow to the head would merely result in more head trauma, and would most likely exacerbate the problem!

What if I were to breathe 100% oxygen?

We breathe air that is 21% oxygen, and we require oxygen to live. So you might think that breathing 100% oxygen would be good for us — but actually it can be harmful. So the short answer is that pure oxygen is generally bad, and sometimes toxic. To understand why, we need to go into some detail. . . .

Your lungs are basically a long series of tubes that branch out from your nose and mouth (from trachea to bronchi to bronchioles) and end in little thin-walled air sacs called *alveoli*. Think of soap bubbles on the end of a straw, and you'll understand alveoli. Surrounding each alveolus are small, thin-walled blood vessels, called pulmonary capillaries. Between the capillaries and the alveolus is a thin wall (about 0.5 microns thick) through which various gases (oxygen, carbon dioxide, nitrogen) pass.

When you inhale, the alveoli fill with air. Because the oxygen concentration is high in the alveoli and low in the blood entering the pulmonary capillaries, oxygen diffuses from the air into the blood. Likewise, because the concentration of carbon dioxide is higher in the blood that's entering the capillary than it is in the alveolar air, carbon dioxide passes from the blood to the alveoli. The nitrogen concentration in the blood and the alveolar air is about the same. The gases exchange across the alveolar wall, and the air inside the alveoli becomes depleted of oxygen and rich in carbon dioxide. When you exhale, you breathe out this carbon dioxide–rich, oxygen-poor air.

Now, what would happen if you breathed 100% oxygen? In guinea pigs exposed to 100% oxygen at normal air pressure for 48 hours, fluid accumulates in the lungs and the epithelial cells lining the alveoli. In addition, the pulmonary capillaries get damaged. A highly reactive form of the oxygen molecule, called the *oxygen free radical*, which destroys proteins and membranes in the

Body and Mind

epithelial cells, probably causes this damage. In humans breathing 100% oxygen at normal pressure, here's what happens:

- Fluid accumulates in the lungs.

- Gas flow across the alveoli slows down, meaning that the person has to breathe more to get enough oxygen.

- Chest pains occur during deep breathing.

- The total volume of exchangeable air in the lung decreases by 17%.

- Mucus plugs local areas of collapsed alveoli — a condition called *atelectasis*. The oxygen trapped in the plugged alveoli gets absorbed into the blood, no gas is left to keep the plugged alveoli inflated, and they collapse. Mucus plugs are normal, but they're cleared by coughing. If alveoli become plugged while breathing air, the nitrogen trapped in the alveoli keeps them inflated.

The astronauts in the Gemini and Apollo programs breathed 100% oxygen at reduced pressure for up to two weeks with no problems. In contrast, when 100% oxygen is breathed under high pressure (more than four times that of atmospheric pressure), acute oxygen poisoning can occur with these symptoms:

- Nausea

- Dizziness

- Muscle twitches

- Blurred vision

- Seizures/convulsions

Such high-oxygen pressures can be experienced by military SCUBA divers using rebreathing devices, divers being treated for the bends in hyperbaric chambers, or patients being treated for acute carbon monoxide poisoning. These patients must be carefully monitored during treatment.

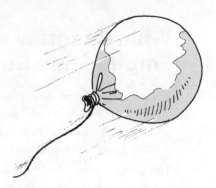

5

Just Plain Odd

✹ What if I threw a penny off the Empire State Building?
• What if people had gills? • What if I tied 150 helium balloons to
my Jack Russell terrier that weighs only 10 pounds — would she
float away in the air? • What if someone released a large amount
of helium into a small office space — would everyone start talking in really high, squeaky voices? • What if I accidentally super-
glued my fingers or lips together? • What if I had earrings or
some other body piercing and forgot to remove the ring before
I had an MRI? • What if I wanted to visit all seven continents in
one day? Is this possible? • What if I were on a roller coaster
going through a loop-the-loop and my safety harness broke?

What if I threw a penny off the Empire State Building?

You might have heard the tale about a person who, standing on the observation deck of the Empire State Building, throws a penny and makes a wish. In the story the penny falls and kills a pedestrian on the sidewalk below.

This is one of those classic urban legends that is untrue, but it contains a grain of truth.

Throwing a penny off the Empire State Building would not kill someone. A penny only weighs about a gram and it tumbles as it falls. Because of the tumbling and the light weight, there is so much air resistance that the penny never really gathers that much speed before it hits its terminal velocity. A gram of weight traveling at a relatively slow speed might hurt a little if it hit you on the head, but it's not going to kill you.

The grain of truth embedded in this urban legend is the fact that falling objects — even ones that seem harmless — can do a lot of damage. That's why people on construction sites wear hard hats. If a big nut or bolt weighing 50 grams (about 1.8 ounces) falls and hits you on the head, it is going to do some serious damage, and depending on the height it falls from, it could definitely kill you if it hit right on top of your skull.

To get an idea of the damage it can do, let's take a look at a bullet. A bullet might weigh 5 to 10 grams, and it leaves the barrel of a gun at anywhere from 800 to 2,000 miles per hour, depending on the type of gun, the type of bullet, and the amount of powder behind the bullet. A 44-caliber bullet weighs about 9 grams. Let's assume it leaves the gun at 1,000 miles per hour. That gives it a muzzle energy of about 300 foot-pounds (1 foot-pound is the amount of energy needed to raise 1 pound 1 foot in the air). Three-hundred foot-pounds of energy is clearly enough to kill someone. Even a third of that is enough to kill someone.

A 1-gram penny falling from the Empire State Building might reach 100 miles per hour. It has a little less than 1 foot-pound of energy when it hits, and just hurts a little.

If a 50-gram nut, or a roll of pennies weighing 50 grams, were to fall from the Empire State Building, it would fall about

1,000 feet. Ignoring air resistance, it would reach a velocity of about 250 miles per hour. That gives it energy of about 100 foot-pounds, which is fatal if it hits you on the head. If you are wearing a hard hat, however, you will survive.

What if people had gills?

In the movie *WaterWorld* with Kevin Costner, Costner's character has a mutation that gives him gills behind the ears. Is this really possible? Could a mutation allow people to swim in the water just like fish, without having to use any sort of SCUBA equipment?

One way to answer that question would be to look at evolution's record on the topic. Every time evolution has put a mammal in the water, whether it's a whale, a porpoise, a walrus, or a manatee, evolution always does it with lungs rather than gills. Evolution often does drastic things to rearrange the rest of the body around the lungs — for example, putting blowholes way back on top of the head in the case of whales — but evolution has never resorted to mammals with gills.

Why is that? The main reason lies in the fact that a mammal's gills would have to be gigantic. Gills work for fish because fish, being cold blooded, don't need that much oxygen. A typical warm-blooded human being might require 15 times more oxygen per pound of body weight than a cold-blooded fish. When swimming, a human being would require even more oxygen than normal. Fish also use their mouths and gill flaps to move large amounts of water through their gills. Sharks and some other fish have to move constantly through the water so that enough water flows over their gills.

Think about how much of a fish's head is consumed by gills. Now imagine a human being with something like 15 times more room devoted to gills and some sort of system to force water over the gill surface. This is why you never see mammals with gills.

What if I tied 150 helium balloons to my Jack Russell terrier that weighs only 10 pounds — would she float away in the air?

Helium has a lifting force of 1 gram per liter. So if you have a balloon that contains 5 liters of helium, the balloon can lift 5 grams.

A normal balloon at an amusement park might be 30 centimeters (about 1 foot) in diameter. To determine how many liters of helium a sphere can hold, use the equation $\frac{4}{3} \times$ pi $\times$ r $\times$ r $\times$ r. The radius of a 30-centimeter-diameter balloon is 15 centimeters, so:

$$\frac{4}{3} \times \text{pi} \times 15 \times 15 \times 15 = 14{,}137 \text{ cubic centimeters} = 14 \text{ liters}$$

So a normal amusement park balloon can lift about 14 grams, assuming that the weight of the balloon itself and the string is negligible.

If your dog weighs 10 pounds, that's about 4,536 grams. 4,536 grams ÷ 14 grams per balloon = 324 balloons to match your dog's weight. As you can see, then, the answer is no. You would need at least 174 more balloons to have lift-off.

Now, let's say that instead of using a lot of little balloons, you go to an army surplus store and you buy one balloon with a diameter of 3 meters (about 10 feet). It can hold

$$\frac{4}{3} \times \text{pi} \times 150 \times 150 \times 150 = 14{,}137{,}000 \text{ cubic centimeters} = 14{,}137 \text{ liters}$$

So, with just one of these big balloons, your dog, along with two other 10-pound terriers, could be soaring to new heights in no time. Of course, this is certainly something we would not recommend trying!

What if someone released a large amount of helium into a small office space — would everyone start talking in really high, squeaky voices?

Talking is an amazing skill. When you talk, your voice starts with a stream of air flowing up your trachea from your lungs. The air passes between the vibrating vocal chords in your larynx. The sound produced consists of a fundamental frequency, which determines your voice's pitch, and harmonics of this frequency. For adult males and females, the average frequencies of the fundamentals are 130 hertz and 205 hertz, respectively.

The sound that comes out of your mouth gets modified by the shape of your throat, mouth, and nasal cavities and by movements of your tongue and lips.

One of the things that determines your voice's pitch is the speed of sound. In air, sound travels at 330 meters per second (m/s) or so. It turns out that the speed of sound in helium is almost three times faster — nearly 900 m/s. So, when you talk with helium in your lungs, all of the sound waves travel nearly three times faster through your throat, mouth, and nasal cavities, creating a pitch that is nearly three times higher. Presto — you sound like Donald Duck!

At a pressure of one atmosphere, with pure helium in your vocal tract instead of air, the pitch of your voice will be about two and a half octaves higher than usual. It's highly unlikely that someone would be able to release enough helium into an office space to create a situation where everyone would be breathing in pure helium. Even if it were possible, the people would suffocate very quickly.

But what if there was a mixture of helium and oxygen — would that have a discernable impact on everyone's voices? It turns out that if you're breathing a helium-oxygen mixture containing 68% helium by volume, the pitch of your voice does increase — but only by one and a half octaves. Therefore, if someone were to release enough helium into the office so that the "air" contained 68% helium by volume, there would be a noticeable lift to

everyone's voices. However, it wouldn't be that same familiar
squeaky effect that sucking the helium out of a balloon produces.

What if I accidentally super-glued my fingers or lips together?

It's no surprise that this actually happens — probably more often
than you might think.

Super glue definitely deserves its name — a 1-square-inch bond
can hold more than a ton. So, what if you find yourself in a
super-sticky situation?

The main ingredient in super glue is cyanoacrylate ($C_5H_5NO_2$,
for you chemistry buffs). Cyanoacrylate is an acrylic resin that
cures (forms its strongest bond) almost instantly. The only trigger
it requires is the hydroxyl ions in water, which is convenient since
virtually any object you might wish to glue will have at least trace
amounts of water on its surface. Air also contains water in the
form of humidity.

White glues, such as Elmer's, bond by solvent evaporation. The
solvent in Elmer's all-purpose school glue is water. When the
water evaporates, the polyvinylacetate latex that has spread into a
material's crevices forms a flexible bond. Super glue, on the other
hand, undergoes a process called *anionic polymerization*. The
chemical process of polymerization produces a certain amount of
heat. If a large enough amount of super glue makes contact with
your skin, it can actually cause burns.

Cyanoacrylate molecules start linking up when they come into
contact with water, and they whip around in chains to form a
durable plastic mesh. The glue thickens and hardens until the
thrashing molecular strands can no longer move.

Let's say you're repairing some broken pottery, and before you
can say "Whoops," you've glued your index finger to your thumb!
The recommended first-aid treatment for this is

1. Scrape off any excess glue. Don't use cloth or tissue — a
   chemical reaction between the fabric and glue could potentially cause burns or smoke.

2. Soak the bonded fingers in a bath of warm, soapy water.

3. Do not try forcing the fingers apart, or you will tear the skin.

4. After soaking, use some kind of dull, rounded utensil to carefully wedge the fingers apart.

5. If you see no immediate success with this, drop a little acetone (found in nail polish remover) on the area. Again try wedging the digits apart.

At first, the thought of someone getting super glue on his or her mouth seems pretty outlandish. But let's face it — a lot of us have a bad habit of using our teeth to wrench or twist off particularly stubborn caps. Say you do that with the top of the tube of glue and, presto, you've given an entirely new meaning to the phrase "zip it." In order to unzip those lips, your options on what to do are a little more limited:

1. Since you're dealing with an area on the face, do not use acetone.

2. Using a wide-brimmed coffee cup or a bowl, immerse your mouth in hot water.

3. You will also want to dampen the bonded skin from the inside of your mouth as much as possible.

4. Once you sense a loosening of the grip, use a dull, rounded utensil to wedge your mouth open. Be careful not to force it, or you will tear the skin.

If you think cyanoacrylate's ability to repair broken knickknacks is super, wait until you hear about its other tricks. An interesting application is the use of cyanoacrylate to close wounds in place of stitches. Researchers found that by changing the type of alcohol in super glue — from ethyl or methyl alcohol to butyl or octyl — the compound becomes less toxic to human tissue. Physicians aren't the only healthcare providers using cyanacrylate as a pharmacological fixative for their patients. Veterinarians use it too.

What if I had earrings or some other body piercing and forgot to remove the jewelry before I had an MRI?

Magnetic resonance imaging (MRI) provides an unparalleled view inside the human body. The level of detail that MRI provides is extraordinary. MRI is the method of choice for the diagnosis of many types of injuries and conditions because of the incredible ability to tailor the exam to the particular medical question being asked.

The biggest and most important component in an MRI system is the magnet. The magnet in an MRI system is rated using a unit of measure known as a *tesla*. Another unit of measure commonly used with magnets is the *gauss* (1 tesla = 10,000 gauss). The magnets in use today in MRI are in the 0.5-tesla to 2.0-tesla range, or 5,000 to 20,000 gauss. Magnetic fields greater than 2 tesla have not been approved for use in medical imaging, though much more powerful magnets — up to 60 tesla — are used in research. Compared with the earth's 0.5-gauss magnetic field, you can see how incredibly powerful these magnets are.

Because of the power of these magnets, the MRI suite can be a very dangerous place if strict precautions are not observed. Metal objects can become dangerous projectiles if they are taken into the scan room. For example, paper clips, pens, keys, scissors, hemostats, stethoscopes, and any other small objects can be pulled out of pockets and off the body without warning, at which point they fly toward the opening of the magnet (where the patient is placed) at very high speeds, posing a threat to everyone in the room. Credit cards, bank cards, and anything else with magnetic encoding will be erased by most MRI systems.

The magnetic force exerted on an object increases exponentially as it nears the magnet. Imagine standing 15 feet (4.6 meters) away from the magnet with a large pipe wrench in your hand. You might feel a slight pull. Take a couple of steps closer, and that pull is much stronger. When you get to within 3 feet (1 meter) of the magnet, the wrench likely is pulled from your grasp. The more mass an object has, the more dangerous it can be — the force with which it is attracted to the magnet is much stronger. Mop buckets, vacuum cleaners, IV poles, oxygen tanks, patient stretchers, heart monitors, and countless other objects have all been pulled into the magnetic fields of MRI machines. Smaller objects can usually be pulled free of the magnet by hand. Large ones may have to be pulled away with a winch, or the magnetic field may even have to be shut down.

Prior to a patient or support staff member being allowed into the scan room, he or she is thoroughly screened for metal objects — and not just external objects. Often, patients have implants inside them that make it very dangerous for them to be in the presence of a strong magnetic field. Metallic fragments in the eye are very dangerous because moving those fragments could cause eye damage or blindness. People with pacemakers cannot be scanned or even go near the scanner because the magnet can cause the pacemaker to malfunction. Aneurysm clips in the brain can be very dangerous, as the magnet can move them, causing them to tear the very artery they were placed on to repair.

As you can see, MRI magnetic fields are incredibly strong. If a piece of metal were missed during your screening, it could cause a problem. Jewelry flying from your body and into the MRI machine is entirely possible.

What if I wanted to visit all seven continents in one day? Is this possible?

First, you must think about a few things. Where are you going? Where will you start your trip? Does "in one day" simply mean a 24-hour time period? Or do you want to use a broader sense — and pay attention to the date, not the actual passage of time? And last but not least, what mode of transportation should you use?

Your travel itinerary would include visits to each of the following continents:

- Africa
- Antarctica
- Asia

- Australia
- Europe
- North America
- South America

You'd be covering an incredible distance on your journey. At first blush, this seems impossible. But there are two ways you might manage a trip like this. You can use an extremely fast mode of transportation, like the Concorde, or you can work with the interpretation of "in one day." We'll take a look at the Concorde in just a minute, but first let's talk about an interesting loophole.

Everyone on the planet wants the sun to be at its highest point in the sky (crossing the meridian) at noon. If there were just one set time for the entire world, this would be impossible because the earth rotates 15 degrees every hour. Therefore, the world is set up in time zones. The idea behind multiple time zones is to divide the world into 24 15-degree slices and set the clocks accordingly in each zone. All of the people in a given zone set their clocks the same way, and each zone is 1 hour different from the next. If you pay attention to the time zones, you can use them to your benefit when planning your trip. It will help you accomplish your task if you interpret "in one day" to mean the date of your trip, not simply a 24-hour time period. Using the time zones, you can start somewhere in the east and move west. As you travel, you will actually be gaining additional hours for your journey because of the time change.

If time weren't an issue, you could choose between taking a boat or a plane or use a combination of the two. But, since planes are definitely faster, that's what you should use. A Boeing 747 aircraft cruises at about 560 mph (901 kph, or Mach 0.84). However, the Concorde cruises at 1,350 mph (2,172 kph, or Mach 2) — about 2½ times faster than a 747. In November of 1986, a British Airways Concorde flew 28,238 miles — an around-the-world trip — in just under 30 hours.

The cost of a Concorde flight from London to New York is about $5,100 one way. Even though chartering a Concorde for your trip would probably cost several million dollars, for the benefit of this question we'll assume you have the money.

We've established that traveling a certain way will give us more time to work with, so the route will move east to west. You will start on Antarctica and fly to the Australian continent and then on to Asia. From there you will travel to the European continent and move to the continent of Africa. After that, it's on to the South American continent, with your final flight taking you to North America. The actual journey, from country to country, is as follows:

McMurdo Station, Antarctica to Christchurch, New Zealand

Christchurch, New Zealand to Bangkok, Thailand

Bangkok, Thailand to Paris, France

Paris, France to Ouagadougou, Burkina Faso

Ouagadougou, Burkina Faso to Caracas, Venezuela

Caracas, Venezuela to Dallas, Texas

It turns out that the most difficult leg of the journey to plan is the first flight. Although there are more than 20 dedicated landing strips on Antarctica, they are mostly gravel or ice-encrusted runways and would not accommodate a Concorde. The U.S. Air Force and the Royal New Zealand Air Force travel to and from a research area in Antarctica known as McMurdo Station. The weather can make take-offs and landings pretty difficult. So difficult in fact, that some flights from Christchurch to McMurdo Station are called "boomerangs" because they have to turn around mid-flight due to inclement weather. As you would imagine, the duration of flights varies depending on the weather, but the average flight takes between 6 and 7 hours. McMurdo Station and Christchurch observe the same time. So let's say you take off from McMurdo at 10:30 a.m. — you will arrive in Christchurch at 5:00 p.m.

From this point on, let's say you've chartered a Concorde. The following grid shows the local departure time, duration of the flight, the time difference, and arrival time for each leg of the journey. We were able to determine the duration of the flights based on the nautical miles between destinations and the fact that a Concorde can travel approximately 1,173 knots in 1 hour. For example, there are 5,082.35 nautical miles between Bangkok International Airport in Thailand and Charles de Gaulle airport in Paris, France. So:

5,082.35 ÷ 1,173 = 4.33, or 4 hours and 20 minutes

Leg	Local Departure Time	Duration of Flight	Time Difference	Local Arrival Time
McMurdo to Christchurch	10:30 a.m.	6 hrs, 30 min	0 hours	5:00 p.m.
Christchurch to Bangkok	6:00 p.m.	4 hrs, 45 min	6 hours	4:45 p.m.
Bangkok to Paris	5:30 p.m.	4 hrs, 20 min	6 hours	4:00 p.m.
Paris to Ouagadougou	5:00 p.m.	2 hrs, 10 min	1 hour	6:10 p.m.
Ouagadougou to Caracas	7:00 p.m.	3 hrs, 35 min	4 hours	6:35 p.m.
Caracas to Dallas	7:30 p.m.	2 hrs, 10 min	2 hours	7:40 p.m.

It's easy to see that it is possible to travel to each continent in one day. In fact, if you look at the total airtime (23 hours and 40 minutes), you'll discover that, were it possible to land and take off with about a 3- or 4-minute turnaround, you would even make it in under the 24-hour time period, too. But, landings and take-offs do take more time than 3 or 4 minutes!

Using the time zones and the top speed transportation of the Concorde, it almost seems too easy. With this scenario, you've even got time for a quick venture out of the plane for a photo or two. But what if you could only use a 747?

Leg	Local Departure Time	Duration of Flight	Time Difference	Local Arrival Time
McMurdo to Christchurch	12:30 a.m.	6 hrs, 30 min	0 hours	7:00 a.m.
Christchurch to Bangkok	7:30 a.m.	11 hours	6 hours	12:30 p.m.
Bangkok to Paris	1:00 p.m.	11 hours	6 hours	6:00 p.m.
Paris to Ouagadougou	6:30 p.m.	5 hours	1 hour	10:30 p.m.
Ouagadougou to Caracas	11 p.m.	8 hours	4 hours	3:00 a.m.
Caracas to Dallas	3:30 a.m.	4 hrs, 30 min	2 hours	6:00 a.m.

From this, you can see that it's just not possible to make a trip of this kind in one day on a 747.

What if I were on a roller coaster going through a loop-the-loop and my safety harness broke?

A roller coaster loop-the-loop is a sort of centrifuge. As you approach the loop, your velocity is straight ahead of you. But the track keeps the coaster car, and therefore your body, from traveling along this straight path. The car starts to turn upward and your velocity is trying to carry you straight ahead. The force of your inertia pushes you into the car floor. This creates a sort of false gravity pulling you toward the bottom of the car when you're upside down. You need a safety harness for security, but in most loop-the-loops, you would stay in the car whether you had a harness or not.

As you move around the loop, the net force acting on your body is constantly changing. At the very bottom of the loop, the acceleration force is pushing you down in the same direction as gravity. Since both forces push you in the same direction, you feel especially heavy at this point. As you move straight up the loop, gravity is pulling you into the back of your seat while the acceleration force is pushing you into the floor. You feel the gravity pulling you into your seat, but (if your eyes are still open) you can see that the ground is no longer where it should be.

At the top of the loop, when you're completely upside down, gravity is pulling you out of your seat, toward the ground, but the stronger acceleration force is pushing you into your seat, toward the sky. Since the two forces pushing you in opposite directions are nearly equal, your body might feel very light. It depends on how fast the car is going and how tight the loop is. As you come out of the loop and level out, you become heavy again.

The loop-the-loop is amazing because it crams so much into such a short length of track. The varying forces put your body through a whole range of sensations in a matter of seconds. While these forces are shaking up all the parts of your body, your eyes see the entire world flip upside down. To many coaster riders, this moment at the top of the loop, when you're light as a feather and all you can see is the sky, is the best part of the whole ride.

6

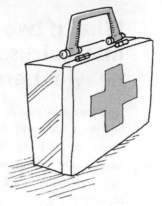

Survival Guide

🌟 What if two people stumbled into quicksand — would the heavier person sink faster? • What if I were on an elevator and the cable broke? • What if I accidentally zapped someone with my stun gun? • What if I accidentally ended up locked in a walk-in freezer? • What if you were stranded several miles off shore in cold weather? • What if I were ice fishing and fell through the ice? • What if someone picked my pocket or stole my wallet? • What if I got to be a contestant on one of those survival game shows and I had to walk on fire or lay on a bed of nails? • What if my SCUBA diving equipment failed?

What if two people stumbled into quicksand — would the heavier person sink faster?

Before we delve into this question, we need to take a look at how quicksand works. When you see quicksand in the movies, a doom-destined hero or heroine is typically being sucked into a huge mass of moving, wet sand. Fortunately, quicksand is not quite the fearsome force of nature that you sometimes see on the big screen.

Quicksand is not a unique type of soil; it is usually just sand or another type of grainy soil. It can occur anywhere under the right conditions, according to Denise Dumouchelle, a geologist with the Unites States Geological Survey. A good example is sand at the beach. Think about the wet sand just at the edge of the surf. You look at it and it looks solid. But when you tap it with your big toe, it jiggles. Quicksand is basically just ordinary sand with reduced friction between sand particles. The "quick" in "quicksand" refers to how easily the sand shifts.

Two things can make sand become quick:

- **Flowing underground water:** The water seeps up into the sand, creating a tiny pocket between each sand granule. As the sand becomes saturated with water, the friction between the sand particles is reduced. The sand takes on a fluid-like quality.

- **Earthquakes:** The immense force of the earthquake agitates the sand or dirt, sifting it apart, so that friction between the particles is reduced. The affected area becomes unstable, causing buildings or other objects on that surface to sink or fall over.

Okay, so now we know how it works — but what happens when two people stumble into some quicksand? The average human body has a density of 62.4 pounds per cubic foot (1 g/cm^3) and is able to float on water. If you have a low percentage of body fat, you are going to be denser, but the air trapped in your lungs will still let you float. Quicksand is denser than water — it has a density of about 125 pounds per cubic foot (2 g/cm^3) — which means you can float more easily on quicksand than on water.

The key is to not panic. Most people who drown in quicksand, or in any liquid for that matter, usually panic and begin flailing their arms and legs.

The most common misconception about quicksand is that it is some kind of living, bottomless pit of sand that actually pulls you down into it. If you step into quicksand, you actually won't be sucked down. However, your movements can cause you to dig yourself deeper into it. According to Dumouchelle, once you've stepped into quicksand, it's your weight that initially causes you to sink. So at first the heavier person might sink more quickly. But once each victim is in up to his or her knees or so, weight doesn't really matter. If a person has a higher percentage of body fat, it is possible he or she will have a very slight advantage and be more buoyant — and will float to the top more quickly.

The worst thing to do is to thrash around in quicksand and move your arms and legs through the mixture. You will only succeed in forcing yourself further down into the liquid sandpit. The best thing to do if you fall into deep quicksand is to make slow movements and bring yourself to the surface, then just lie back. You'll float to a safe level. This approach works best in quicksand that is fairly well saturated.

The sand-to-water ratio of quicksand can vary, causing some quicksand to be less able to support weight. So, if you find yourself in sand that is less saturated (think of concrete) there is a better method to try.

One of the most common reactions, once a person finds his or her foot stuck, is to shift weight to the other foot. At this point, a sort of seesaw motion happens — with the person alternating weight back and forth trying to get a foot out of the quicksand. This movement actually worsens the predicament. What you should do instead is fall forward and try to spread the weight of your body over a large area of ground. Continue to work at freeing your foot, using slow motions so that you don't work your foot in deeper. Once you've pulled your foot out, roll away from the area, jump up very quickly, and sprint to solid ground.

There have been many cases where people have gotten their legs trapped in quicksand and have not been able to escape on their own. The sand has to be at just the right moisture for this to happen and the person has to be at least thigh-deep with both legs. Extricating a person from this takes at least two passersby, if not a full-fledged rescue team.

What if I were on an elevator and the cable broke?

In the world of action movies, any elevator is never far from plummeting dozens of stories and disintegrating in a ball of fire (and probably a gratuitous explosion or two) at the bottom of the shaft. Fortunately, the elevators of the real world are a bit more stable. In fact, modern elevators have so many safety features that such a situation is virtually unheard of. It has happened at least once, when a plane hit the Empire State Building in 1945. Amazingly, the sole passenger, an elevator operator named Betty Oliver, survived the 75-story fall.

In a roped elevator system, steel ropes are bolted to the car. (Elevator engineers call them *ropes* rather than *cables* to distinguish them from electrical cables.) These ropes are looped over a sort of pulley at the top of the elevator shaft. This device is called a *sheave*. Grooves along the sheave grip the steel ropes. An electric motor rotates the sheave, and as it moves, so do the attached ropes. The sheave-and-rope system raises and lowers the car, which rides along steel rails inside the elevator shaft.

Each elevator rope is made from several lengths of steel material wound around one another. These ropes very rarely snap, and inspectors regularly examine them for wear and tear. Elevators are almost always built with multiple ropes (between four and eight). In the unlikely event that one of the ropes were to snap, the rest would hold the elevator up. In fact, one rope by itself would be strong enough to hold the elevator. The short answer, then, is that nothing would happen if a rope (or even two or three ropes) were to break.

But suppose all of the ropes snapped at the same time. In this scenario, the elevator's safeties would kick in. Safeties are braking systems on the elevator car that clamp onto the rails running up and down the elevator shaft. Typically, safeties are activated by a mechanical speed governor.

The speed governor is a pulley reel that rotates when the elevator moves. When the speed governor spins too fast, the centrifugal force of the rotation drives two pivoting flyweights outward against a lever that activates the braking system. The braking system slows the car gradually before stopping it completely. High-rise elevators typically have additional independent braking systems that automatically slow the car when it reaches the top and bottom of the shaft or if the power cuts off.

If all this were to fail, and the car were to plummet down the shaft, things could get pretty weird. In a free fall (a fall factoring in only the force of gravity), all objects fall toward the center of the earth, accelerating at a rate of 9.8 meters per second^2. If the elevator is in a free fall, you would be in a free fall also, separate of the elevator's motion. Since the floor would be falling out from under you at the same rate you were falling toward the earth, you would feel like you were weightless. You could push off the floor, and you would "float" in the middle of the elevator car.

But if the car fell all the way to the bottom of the shaft, you would quickly discover that you weren't actually weightless. When the car stopped moving, it would suddenly become stable ground again, but you would still be falling. You would hit the car floor very hard, as if you had jumped down an empty shaft. Additionally, the car would fall apart on impact. In other words, your chances of survival wouldn't be all that great if the elevator had fallen more than a few floors.

But, as it turns out, a plummeting elevator car would not actually be in a free fall. Friction from the rails along the shaft and pressure from the air underneath the car would slow it down considerably. You would feel lighter than normal, since the floor was falling out from under you, but gravity would be accelerating you more rapidly than the car, so you would stay on the floor. The floor would slow your dissent, so the force of a sudden impact wouldn't be quite so severe. If the car fell far enough, however, the impact at the bottom could still kill you.

But as luck would have it, the elevator car probably wouldn't come to an abrupt stop. Most rope elevator systems have a built-in shock absorber at the bottom of the shaft. This shock absorber, typically a piston in an oil-filled cylinder, would cushion the impact of a falling elevator car. You would have a very good chance of surviving this cushioned impact.

If you were to find yourself in such a harrowing fall, the best course of action would probably be to lie down on the floor. This would stabilize you and spread out the force of the impact. No single part of your body would take the brunt of the blow.

Don't bother jumping

There is a pervasive theory that if you were to jump immediately before the elevator car hit, you would stand a better chance, since your jump would help counteract your downward momentum. Even if you could perfectly time such a leap (which would be nearly impossible), it wouldn't do you much good. It would only diminish your downward momentum by a very small fraction — you're only jumping up a little, but you're falling down a lot. You would hit the floor with roughly the same force.

What if I accidentally zapped someone with my stun gun? What happens when a person gets zapped?

On the old *Star Trek* series, Captain Kirk and his crew never left the ship without their trusty phasers. One of the coolest things about these weapons was the stun setting.

We're still a ways off from this futuristic weaponry, but millions of police officers, soldiers, and ordinary citizens do carry real-life stun weapons to protect against personal attacks.

We tend to think of electricity as a harmful force to our bodies. If lightning strikes you or you stick your finger in an electrical outlet, the current can maim or even kill you. But in smaller doses, electricity is harmless. In fact, it is one of the most essential elements in your body. You need electricity to do just about anything.

When you want to make a sandwich, for example, your brain sends an impulse down a nerve cell toward the muscles in your arm. The electrical signal tells the nerve cell to release a *neurotransmitter,* which is a communication chemical, to the muscle cells. Neurotransmitters tell the muscles to contract or expand in just the right way to put your sandwich together. When you pick up the sandwich, the sensitive nerve cells in your hand send messages to the brain, telling you what the sandwich feels like. When you bite into it, your mouth sends signals to your brain to tell you how it tastes.

In this way, the different parts of your body use electricity to communicate with one another. This is actually a lot like a telephone system or the Internet. Specific patterns of electricity are transmitted to deliver recognizable messages.

The basic idea of a stun gun is to disrupt this communication system. Stun guns generate a high-voltage, low-amperage electrical charge. In simple terms, this means that the charge has a lot of pressure behind it, but not that much intensity. When you press the stun gun against someone and hold the trigger, the charge passes into that person's body. Since it has a fairly high voltage, the charge will flow through heavy clothing and skin. But at around 3 milliamps, the charge is not intense enough to damage the person's body, unless it is applied for extended periods of time.

The charge does dump a lot of confusing information into the person's nervous system, however. The charge combines with the electrical signals from the person's brain. This is like running an outside current into a phone line: The original signal is mixed in with random noise, making it very difficult to decipher any messages. With the stun gun generating a ton of "noise," the person has a very hard time telling his or her muscles to move, and he or she may become confused and unbalanced. He or she is partially paralyzed, temporarily.

The current may be generated with a pulse frequency that mimics the body's own electrical signals. In this case, the current will tell the person's muscles to do a great deal of work in a short amount of time. The action in the muscles is actually happening at a cellular level, so you couldn't really see the person twitching or shaking — the signal doesn't direct the work toward any particular movement. The work doesn't do anything but deplete the person's energy reserves, leaving him or her too weak to move (which is the whole idea, as you would normally be using a stun gun against an attacker).

A stun gun's effectiveness can vary depending on the particular gun model, the size of the person being zapped, and the duration of the actual zap. If you use the gun for half a second, a painful jolt will startle the person. If you zap him or her for one or two seconds, he or she should experience muscle spasms and become dazed. And if you zap the person for more than three seconds, he or she will become unbalanced and disoriented and may lose muscle control. However, determination can be a mitigating factor. Determined attackers with a certain physiology may keep coming despite any shock.

What if I accidentally ended up locked in a walk-in freezer?

It is way past midnight and it's been a really long night at the restaurant where you work. You only need to repair that broken shelf in the walk-in freezer and then you can go home. After you enter the frigid air, you decide it might be a good idea to get your sweatshirt — the shelf may take a few minutes to fix. You push the door but nothing happens. Then you try pressing the safety release handle, and you realize the shelf isn't the only item in disrepair. You think, "Now what am I going to do — why did I agree to lock up by myself tonight?" Since you are all alone, there's no point in ringing the safety bell. You glance at your watch and realize it is going to be about six hours before the breakfast crew arrives. . . .

What do you do in a situation like this? First, take a look at your surroundings to see what you're facing:

- The temperature is probably somewhere between 0°F and −10°F (this would meet the FDA requirement for walk-in freezers).
- The ceiling, walls, and door are 4 to 6 inches thick — made of some kind of insulating foam, like urethane, covered in sheets of galvanized steel, stainless steel, or aluminum.
- The floor is also covered in galvanized steel, stainless steel, or aluminum.

- There are stainless steel shelves loaded with plastic bags filled with meat, poultry, fish, and other frozen foodstuffs.
- A single vapor-proof fixture provides dim lighting.
- A row of thick plastic curtains hangs in the doorway.

Basically, you are inside a tightly sealed, extremely cold, giant metal box. You need to worry about

- Hypothermia
- Frostbite
- The air supply

The normal core body temperature of a healthy person is 98.6°F. Hypothermia occurs when a person's body temperature drops significantly below normal:

- Mild hypothermia — core body temperature between 93.2°F and 96.8°F
- Moderate hypothermia — core body temperature between 73.4°F and 89.6°F
- Severe or profound hypothermia — core body temperature between 53.6°F and 68°F

A person suffering from hypothermia will become tired and confused. He or she may experience slowed breathing and speech followed by a loss of feeling or movement of the hands. Persons with severe hypothermia are at high risk for cardiac arrest, and possibly death.

In order to keep hypothermia at bay, you need to maintain your core body temperature. Your best bet is to fashion some kind of protection from the cold.

You lose body heat in a number of ways. You lose heat when you breathe and perspire. Large areas of exposed skin radiate a lot of heat. Heat can also be conducted from your body through contact with cold surfaces such as snow, or, in this case, extremely cold metal. Obviously, you have a limited cache of useful supplies, but all is not lost. You've gone into the walk-in to repair some shelves, so you have a roll of duct tape in your pocket and an all-purpose tool like a Leatherman or Bucktool. Using those resources, you could remove the plastic curtains from the doorway and make a suit or a tent to insulate yourself from the cold. If you do this quickly, you should be able to keep your body temperature close to normal until you are well insulated, especially since you'll be exerting energy to make the suit or tent. You would then want to use any extra plastic or cardboard you might find to make a thick palette to sit on so that you aren't touching the metal floor, which is a good conductor of energy.

To inhibit frostbite, you need to make sure that your extremities are covered and protected from the cold. The plastic tent or suit should help with this. Your head radiates an incredible amount of heat away from your body. So, if your t-shirt is long enough, cut off any extra material from the hem, making sure not to expose any skin, and use the material and some duct tape to make a hat or head wrap and a pair of mittens. This will protect your hands, head, and face from frostbite and will also help limit the amount of heat you are radiating from your body and exhaling as you breathe.

Now that you know what to do about hypothermia and frostbite, what about the air? Let's say you are in a freezer that is 20 by 10 by 8 feet, and it is completely sealed. That means you have 1,600 cubic feet of air to breathe. Initially the air is 20% oxygen and nearly 0% carbon dioxide. Each time you breathe, your body consumes oxygen and releases carbon dioxide. You inhale air that is 20% oxygen and 0% carbon dioxide and exhale air that is about 15% oxygen and 5% carbon dioxide.

A person at rest breathes about 2,800 cubic feet of air per day. If you do the math, you'll see that a person needs about 150 cubic feet of pure oxygen per day. There's 320 cubic feet of pure oxygen in the freezer. People are okay with oxygen concentrations down to 10% or so, so there's enough oxygen to last for about a full day in a freezer this size. No running and jumping around, however — oxygen is precious in an environment like this.

The other side of the coin is carbon dioxide. Once the concentration of carbon dioxide in the air gets above 5%, it is fatal. At 2%, your breathing rate will increase significantly and weakness is obvious. In a freezer this size, too much carbon dioxide is actually a much bigger problem than too little oxygen. After 6 hours, the effects of carbon dioxide poisoning will be noticeable.

Let's say that you're successful with your tent, hat, and mittens. When the morning crew arrives almost 6 hours later, you will probably be flushed, weak, and dizzy or disoriented from the carbon dioxide. Also, at best, you'll almost certainly be suffering from mild hypothermia, so your speech may be slow and you will

have limited control of your hands. You will need fresh air —
perhaps even supplemental oxygen — and treatment for
hypothermia. Even if you aren't exhibiting all of these
symptoms, it's probably best to seek medical attention.

What if you were stranded several miles off shore in cold weather?

It's early November and you and your college roommate are
amazed by the unseasonably good weather. To enjoy the crisp (it's
about 60°F), sunny day, you decide to take your roommate's dad's
new 28-foot sport-cruiser boat out for a day trip on Lake Huron.
Driving the boat is even more fun than you thought it would be.
Before you know it, you've been out for most of the day. Just as
you decide it's time to come back, there's a really loud sound and
suddenly the boat's motor stops. After several attempts to restart
the motor, you realize that it's dead. Great, now you and your
friend are stranded on the boat, it's getting cold, and it will be
dark soon. What are you going to do?

Even though you can see land in the distance, swimming is not
really an option. Although the water isn't too choppy right now,
it is pretty cold. In water temperatures of 40 to 50°F, you can
suffer exhaustion in as little as 30 minutes and develop hypothermia in as little as an hour. Even if you're a good swimmer, you
couldn't expect to go more than about a mile in these conditions
before becoming fatigued. At that point, you would find yourself
too far from the boat to return and still way too far from shore.
As the effects of hypothermia set in, you would pass out and
eventually drown.

The temperature is dropping and it will be dark soon, so you
need to work fast. The things you need to think about right now
are

- Signaling for help
- Water
- Exposure to the elements
- Food

There are several devices that stranded boaters can use to notify people of their situation:

- EPIRB (emergency position indicating radio beacon)
- Dye packs or water markers
- Flares
- Reflective devices such as mirrors or watches
- Horns or other sound alarms

Because it is getting dark, your options are limited, for now, to the EPIRB, flares, and horns.

Both boaters and pilots use EPIRBs. A modern EPIRB is a sophisticated device that contains

- A 5-watt radio transmitter operating at 406 MHz
- A 0.25-watt radio transmitter operating at 121.5 MHz.
- A GPS receiver

Once activated, both of the radios start transmitting. A GOES weather satellite 24,000 or so miles up in space in a geosynchronous orbit can detect the 406 MHz signal. Embedded in the signal is a unique serial number and, if the unit is equipped with a GPS receiver, the exact location of the radio. If the EPIRB is properly registered, the serial number lets the authorities know who owns the EPIRB. Rescuers in planes or boats can home in on the EPIRB using either the 406 MHz or 121.5 MHz signal.

After you have activated the EPIRB, start sounding the horn intermittently. Next, look around the boat for flares. If you have enough, you can set off a flare every 15 minutes in hopes that a passerby might see your distress signal. However, don't waste your flares if it seems too late for other boaters to be out and about. Save them to use when other boats are likely to be nearby. If you haven't been found by morning, you can incorporate other methods into your routine — such as removing the vanity mirror from the bathroom (the head, in nautical terms) to signal others of your trouble.

You're supposed to have between eight and ten 8-ounce glasses of water a day, so that's about 64 ounces, or half a gallon. Your roommate brought a gallon-sized jug of water on board that morning, but he's been drinking it all day. What are you going to do about water? Luckily, the boat you are on probably has a tank.

For a 28-footer, you can expect that there are about 24 to 32 gallons of potable water in the tank. If for some reason the tank is empty, you can look inside the emergency kit that accompanies the life raft for water purification tablets and filters to create your own drinking water.

If you are on the ocean, instead of a lake, and you are lucky, you will have a solar desalination kit. If not, you have a real problem. Never drink seawater, as the salt will only hasten dehydration.

Although you can survive for several days without food, you'll probably want something to eat. After searching the boat, you discover that you've only got a few packages of beef jerky that you brought along for a snack. Instead of giving in to your pangs of hunger by eating all the jerky at once, you can ration out portions for you and your friend and leave some out to use as bait. Using the dental floss you find in the bathroom, along with some discarded fishing hooks, you can fashion a rudimentary system to catch fish.

Now that you have food and water covered, the remaining concern is the weather. If you have one on board, you should listen to the radio to monitor the weather. With or without a weather report, you should anticipate and plan for the worst. In this area, a daytime temperature of 60°F is certainly out of the norm. The average temperature for the month of November in Alpena, Michigan, is

- High — 43°F
- Low — 28°F

This means that overnight temperatures could easily be in the 30s. Factor in the wind chill, and the temperature could feel closer to something in the teens. If you don't find a way to keep warm, you will be at risk for hypothermia. You can use any tarps or canvas you find (remove seat cushion coverings, if necessary) to make a big blanket or tent. You and your friend can huddle together under the blanket or in your improvised tent to stay out of the wind and share body heat. If it is particularly windy or it starts to rain, you can empty out the storage compartment under the bow or huddle up in the bathroom, making sure to take turns going out on deck to look for rescue planes or boats. Have flares handy, so you can signal if someone approaches.

What if I were ice fishing and fell through the ice?

According to the Michigan Department of Natural Resources, approximately two million people brave freezing temperatures and frightening wind chills every winter to go ice fishing. Many of these avid anglers take to the frozen waters of the Great Lakes. In the process, they place themselves in a potentially dangerous situation. Most ice fishermen are aware of this and take many precautions to maintain safety. A few of these precautionary measures are

- Buddy fishing — ice fishing alone is never a good idea
- Checking ahead — being aware of weather and fishing conditions before embarking on a trip
- Wearing a PFD (personal flotation device)
- Looking for an area with at least 3½ to 4 inches of solid, clear, fresh ice
- Notifying friends and family of fishing plans
- Carrying safety gear such as augers, screwdrivers, spikes, and rope

However, no matter how careful you are, accidents do happen. So what if you do fall through the ice while fishing? Basically, there are two things you need to worry about:

- Drowning
- Hypothermia

In all likelihood you are wearing some kind of PFD, so you shouldn't sink below the surface altogether. At this point, your top priority is to get out of the water. Whether you are wearing a flotation device or not, in water temperatures between 32.5°F and 40°F, you have very little time before hypothermia will start to set in. Victims have been known to succumb to hypothermia in as little as 10 to 15 minutes. If you become hypothermic, you will probably pass out and subsequently drown.

Try to remain calm and quickly grab for surface ice in the direction from where you came. The ice behind you is stronger — remember that you just traveled across it. Using your auger or any other sharp object you have, pull yourself onto the ice. Once you are up and out of the water, do not stand up. By keeping your weight distributed evenly over the ice, you have a better chance of not breaking through again. You can either roll or crawl away from the hole. Once you reach safe ice, you are not out of danger yet. You must be treated for hypothermia as soon as possible. Your body temperature will continue to drop as long as you are in a cold environment. Find shelter and dry clothes immediately. You can drink warm non-alcoholic liquids. No matter how tempting, do not drink any alcohol — it dilates your blood vessels and increases heat loss.

Now let's say it's not you, but your fishing buddy who takes a dive. What should you do? Your first instinct will be to run toward him or her to help. Don't do this — you will both end up in the water! Quickly locate the longest thing you have at hand — your auger, some rope, a pole, or branch will do nicely. Then lie down on the ice and stretch the item out toward your friend. After he or she grabs on, pull your friend to safety. If you don't have anything long enough to reach your friend, but there are several people around, you can form a human chain. Everyone should lie flat on the ice, one in front of the other, holding on to the next person's feet until you can reach the victim. Again, your friend will need to seek first aid for hypothermia.

What if someone picked my pocket or stole my wallet?

It's finally here — vacation time. You're off to London to visit your old college roommate. As you stand in the airport waiting in the line for the ticket counter, you daydream about your impending adventure. Suddenly, you are jostled out of your reverie by the couple in front of you. They are arguing rather loudly over whom, out of the hapless duo, was responsible for remembering to bring the tickets. As they scurry off toward the door, you wander back into your dream state until the ticket person summons you with a loud "Next in line, please."

You place your ticket on the counter and are asked for your driver's license or other identification. Oh, no! Your wallet isn't in your jacket pocket. You scramble through your bag, and it isn't there either. You stand at the ticket counter thinking, "I've lost my wallet, what am I going to do now?"

What you don't realize is that the arguing couple and the gentleman standing behind you are responsible for your missing wallet. Schooled in the art of picking pockets, these professional criminals used the element of distraction to relieve you of your wallet and passport in a matter of seconds. So, what should you do if this happens? First, let's take a look at how pickpockets commit the crime to see what you can do to thwart them.

Picking pockets is one of the oldest and most common crimes in the world, and it shows no sign of going out of style any time soon. Most common in metropolitan areas, pickpocketing thrives in heavily populated, loud areas where there is a lot of activity. Places such as airports, train stations, subway platforms, entertainment venues, and parades provide plenty of pickpocketing opportunities. Anyone can be a pickpocket — men, women, children — there is no age limit and no typical "look." Some of the most successful pickpockets are well-dressed, nicely groomed men and women who appear to be white-collar businesspeople.

More often working in groups than not, these people use various techniques to distract you so that you won't be aware of their slight of hand with your valuables. Some of the tactics they use are

- Two or more people will start some type of commotion, while another person surreptitiously removes a wallet and/or jewelry from the victim, or *mark*.

- The pickpocket will "accidentally" bump into you while removing your wallet.

- The pickpocket will pretend to have lost something, maybe a contact lens or some other hard-to-find object, and will rob you while you help with the search.

- A child will appear to be running away from an angry parent and hide behind you for protection. As the parent starts an argument with you, the child secretly snatches your valuables.

Practiced pickpockets are nimble and intelligent. They can easily spot a good mark (an easy victim) in even the biggest of crowds.

However, there are certain precautions you can take to outwit them:

- Always be aware of your surroundings; be suspicious of people who invade your personal space.
- A man should keep his wallet in the most secured part of his clothing — for example, a front pocket in his jeans, with his hand inside the pocket over the wallet.
- A woman carrying a purse should wear it slung across her body with the purse in front and her hands secured over the opening at all times.
- If possible, keep your money separate from your keys, passport, license, and other valuables
- Keep bills separate; have smaller bills handy so that you aren't displaying all of your money each time you pay.
- Don't carry more money or more credit cards than you need for your outing.
- Wear casual clothing that blends with what others are wearing.
- Wear a minimum of jewelry — obvious pieces will attract unwanted attention.

Even cautious people can be taken advantage of from time to time. Suppose someone does manage to nick your wallet. A few simple tactics of your own can keep your losses to a minimum:

- Keep a record at home, or some other safe location, of all the credit cards and bank cards you carry in your wallet. Photocopies are best, and note the appropriate emergency phone number on each photocopy.
- Maintain an updated record of your spending so that, if necessary, you can compare that with recent purchases on your credit cards.
- Don't carry your social security card in your wallet.
- Don't keep personal identification numbers or access codes in your wallet or purse.
- Don't have your social security number or driver's license number printed on your checks.
- Request credit reports from the credit bureaus (Equifax, Trans Union, and Experian) and keep a listing of their toll-free fraud line phone numbers.

Once your wallet is stolen, you will want to do the following as quickly as possible (preferably within the first 24 to 48 hours):

- File a police report in the area where the crime happened.
- Cancel all of the cards in your wallet — credit cards, AAA, movie rental cards, and so on.
- Notify your bank of stolen checks, check cards, and bank cards.
- Contact the credit bureaus and have them flag your credit report.
- Notify the Department of Motor Vehicles and the Social Security Administration that your identification has been stolen.

Identity fraud is a growing concern. Once someone has possession of your driver's license or social security card and some credit cards, it is fairly easy for the criminal to assume your identity to gain new credit and make some hefty purchases in the process. You can have the credit bureaus flag your report with a note stating that your wallet was stolen, you've filed a police report, and if anyone is attempting to gain new credit or make a large purchase using your name, you should be called for verification. By doing this, you will have an easier time getting out of paying the bills that your impersonator may amass.

What if I got to be a contestant on one of those survival game shows and I had to walk on fire or lay on a bed of nails?

Fire walking is one of those odd things that you see on late-night TV and in certain bizarre religious events. What you always see is a glowing bed of burning coals. Fire walkers make their way across the coals as though by magic. How do they do it, and can any normal person do it just as easily?

There are a couple things to notice about every fire walking event you have ever seen:

- First of all, fire walkers are not *fire* walkers. They are really coal walkers. If there were actual flames leaping up in the air, this stunt would not work. The fire is lit well ahead of time to allow the wood to burn down to non-flaming coals.

- You will also notice that the event is always held at night. If it were done during daylight, the bed of coals would look like a bed of ashes. A layer of ash always covers the coals. By doing it at night, the glowing, red light is still visible through the ash.

- Notice that the fire walkers never dawdle. No self-respecting fire walker would run across the coals. That would be undignified. But they certainly are walking briskly. You never see fire walkers standing on the coals.

- Finally, you will notice that fire walking always happens on the coals themselves. You never, for example, see fire walkers cover the bed of coals with metal plates. Walking across red-hot metal plates would create serious injuries, while walking across coals does not.

So what's going on here? Fire walking depends on a combination of poor conduction, insulation, and a short time span.

A wood coal is a poor conductor. It is made up of almost pure carbon and is very light. It takes a relatively long time for heat to transfer from the coal to your skin. If the coal were replaced with red-hot metal, heat transfer would be almost instantaneous, and you would get a severe burn.

Now, add to that the fact that ash is a very good insulator. Coals covered with ash transfer their heat even more slowly.

Then there is the short time span. Heat transfer from a red-hot coal is slow, but it still happens. If you were to stand still on the coals for several seconds, you would definitely get a severe burn. By walking briskly, you limit your contact with individual coals to a very short time span. You also get across the bed of coals very quickly, and that limits your total amount of coal time. Your feet never get hot enough to burn.

If asked to walk across coals on a survival show, make sure that they are truly coals — no flames. Make sure there's a little ash. And then walk as quickly as you can to the other side. You'll get that million-dollar check in no time!

The bed of nails is even simpler. For the sake of calculation, let's say that you are 6 feet tall and 14 inches wide. That means that one side of your body has over 1,000 square inches of surface area. A typical bed will have the nails spaced an inch apart, or even closer. When you lie on the bed, there are about 1,000 points of contact between you and the nails. If you weigh 200 pounds, then each nail point is supporting only one fifth of a pound, or perhaps 3 ounces, which just isn't very much. There's a classic demonstration where a balloon is pressed onto a bed of nails without popping. The total pressure is spread over so many points that no one point can puncture the balloon.

The main problem with a bed of nails is getting on and off. If you aren't careful, then the initial point of contact can have a small surface area supporting a large amount of weight. As you are getting on, support most of your weight with your hands and feet on the floor and ease your weight onto the nails as the sur-face area in contact with them increases. Wearing heavy jeans also helps!

The other problem is your head. Your head is heavy and it's not flat, so only a few nails are touching your scalp. It is very easy to do damage to your head on a bed of nails if you are not careful. The best solution is to use a pillow! If the game show doesn't let you do that, you should use your neck muscles to keep your head off of the nails.

What if my SCUBA diving equipment failed?

Diving equipment failure — yikes! While we all agree this would be a frightening experience, it's usually not as dire as it sounds. When you hear about a diving incident, it most often involves a malfunctioning regulator or a tank low on air. There are two things you need to worry about if your equipment fails:

- Your lungs
- The bends

Typical recreational SCUBA divers breathe either compressed air (78% nitrogen, 21% oxygen) or an oxygen-enriched, nitrogen-oxygen combination called nitrox (64 to 68% nitrogen, 32 to 36% oxygen). The gas is contained in a cylinder that you carry on your back. You cannot breathe directly out of the tank because the high pressure would damage your lungs. Therefore, the cylinder is fitted with a regulator. The regulator does two things: It reduces the pressure from the tank to a safe level for you to inhale, and it supplies air on demand.

To accomplish these tasks, regulators have two stages:

- First stage — The first stage attaches to the cylinder. It reduces the pressure from the tank (3000 psi, or 204 atmospheres) to an intermediate pressure (140 psi, or 9.5 atmospheres).

- Second stage — The second stage is connected to the first stage by a hose. It reduces the pressure from the intermediate pressure to ambient water pressure (such as 1 to 5 atmospheres, depending on depth). The second stage also supplies air, either only when you inhale (typical operation) or continuously (emergency operation).

So what would happen if your regulator were to malfunction or your tank ran out of air? Obviously, when the air stops, your first instinct will be to head straight for the surface. There are two things to keep in mind.

As you ascend back to the surface, the air in your lungs will expand. In order to keep your lungs from expanding too quickly or too much, you need to exhale as you float to the surface. Think about a balloon. Say you take a blown-up balloon with you as you dive 30 feet below the ocean's surface. The balloon will deflate to about half its capacity by the time you reach your destination because of the pressure of all that water pushing down on it. As you go back to the surface, it will expand. Now let's say you took an empty balloon down 30 feet and somehow inflated it to normal size down there. Then you brought it back to the surface with you. What happens? It expands beyond its capacity and bursts. The same thing would happen to your lungs if you don't exhale constantly. To keep the balloon or your lungs from exploding, you would need to constantly release air to keep them from becoming overfull. If you exhale and rise no faster than the bubbles from your exhalation do, you should be okay.

The other thing you have to worry about, depending on how deep you are when you run out of air, is the *bends*.

The air we breathe is a mixture of mostly nitrogen (78%) and oxygen (21%). When you inhale air, your body consumes the oxygen, replaces some of it with carbon dioxide, and does nothing with the nitrogen. At normal atmospheric pressure, some nitrogen and oxygen is dissolved in the fluid portions of your blood and tissues.

As you descend under the water, the pressure on your body increases, so more nitrogen and oxygen dissolve in your blood. Your tissues consume most of the oxygen, but the nitrogen remains dissolved. All this dissolved nitrogen is where the bends come from.

If you ascend rapidly, the nitrogen comes out of your blood quickly, forming bubbles. It's like opening a can of soda: You hear the hiss of the high-pressure gas and you see the bubbles caused by the gas rapidly coming out of solution. This is what happens in your blood and tissues if you come up too fast. You get the bends (which is also called decompression sickness) when nitrogen bubbles form in your system and block tiny blood vessels. This can lead to heart attacks, strokes, ruptured blood vessels in the lungs, and joint pain (one of the first symptoms of decompression sickness is a tingling sensation in your limbs).

The best way to avoid decompression sickness is to follow the no-decompression depths and bottom times provided by dive tables. If you violate the no-decompression limits, you have to stay underwater longer, for various times at preset depths (determined by dive tables), to allow the nitrogen to come out of your system slowly. This obviously presents problems because you're out of air. So what do you do? The only thing you may be able to do is come up, get another tank, and then immediately dive back down to a safe depth. But if you are near shore, you may be able to go to a decompression chamber instead, and that is much safer.

7

Dollars and Cents

✿ What if I saved a quarter ($.25) every day of my life from the day I was born? • What if I won the lottery? • What if I had to file bankruptcy? • What if I have twins and want to send them to an Ivy League school? • What if I were president of the United States? Would I be the highest paid person in the U.S.? • What if I purchased ten shares of stock when Microsoft first went public? • What if I wrote a bad check?

What if I saved a quarter ($.25) every day of my life from the day I was born?

This is an interesting question because almost anyone can afford a quarter a day. There are several possible scenarios. The amount of savings you can accumulate depends on two main factors: your age and the way you save the money. Obviously, there would be a vast difference in your savings depending on whether you put the quarters into a piggy bank or put them into CDs (not the musical kind) or stocks.

Let's assume your parents start this fiscal ritual and you carry on until your fiftieth birthday. There are 365 days in a year, so that's a quarter every day for 18,250 days. If you merely placed the coins in a piggy bank you would have $4,562.50 at the end of 50 years.

That doesn't seem like enough money for all that effort. You see this early on — say at age 8 — but you're not a risk taker. The local credit union offers 4.5% interest on a money market account with a minimum balance of $500. You have $730 to deposit, and you'll be depositing your regular savings of a quarter a day once per month. The great thing about the money market account is that it compounds your interest monthly.

When you first deposit your savings into the money market account, you have $730 (which is called the principal). The next month when you go to make your monthly deposit, you will have the original $730, plus the interest accumulated for that month, plus your new deposit of $7.50 (assuming there are 30 days in a month). You can use the following formula to calculate how much money you will have after this first month:

Principal + (Principal × Monthly Interest) + Monthly Contributions = Future Value

730 + (730 × .38%) + 7.50 = 740.24

The next month you would have even more principal — $740.24, to be exact. So, after two months you would have

740.24 + (740.24 × .38%) + 7.50 = 760.83

You would continue to figure out this formula for 502 more months since there are 504 months in 42 years. At the end of all that calculating, you would figure out that by the time you are 50 years old, using the money market account, you would have saved $16,313.23 — almost four times as much as using a piggy bank!

If you want to earn even more, you can take a chance and invest your money in the stock market. Expecting normal gains and losses over the 42-year period, you could expect an average interest rate of around 8%. Based on the same method of calculation above, you can expect a savings of $52,419.09 by your fiftieth birthday — not a bad present for saving a bunch of quarters!

What if I won the lottery?

In the United States, 37 states and the District of Columbia (Washington, D.C.) have lotteries. A lottery is a form of gambling that is run by the state. Most states have several different games, including instant win scratch-off games, daily games, and games where you have to pick three or four numbers. But the game with the biggest jackpot is almost always Lotto. This game usually involves picking the correct six numbers from a set of balls, with each ball numbered from 1 to 50 (some games use more or less than 50).

Okay, let's say you picked the right six numbers, and you won a $10 million jackpot — you're going to get $10 million, right? Actually, no. You'll probably only end up with about $2.5 million. Where does all the money go?

We'll use the New York Lotto as an example, as it's one of the largest in the country. When you buy a New York Lotto ticket, you have to choose between receiving your winnings in a lump sum or in a series of annual payments, and you can't change your mind later.

If you chose annual payments when you bought the ticket, what you are really going to win is a series of 26 yearly payments that add up to $10 million. You would receive the first payment for 2.5% of the total, or $250,000, two weeks after you submit the winning ticket (but remember, some taxes would be withheld from each check). One year later, you would receive a check for 2.6%, or $260,000. Each year, the amount of the check goes up by a tenth of a percent; the last payment is for 5%, or $500,000.

In order to guarantee that the funds for all of these payments are available, the New York Lottery buys special U.S. Treasury Bonds called STRIPS (Separate Trading of Registered Interest and Principal of Securities). Also known as zero-coupon bonds, these bonds pay a certain amount of money when they mature. For instance, in March 2001, you could buy a zero-coupon bond that would be worth $1,000 in 10 years for about $610. The further in the future that the bond matures, the less it costs you today. A bond maturing in 25 years for $1,000 would only cost about $260 today. If you do the math, you find out that if you invested the $260 at about 5.7% interest, in 25 years it would be worth $1,000.

When a winner claims his prize, the New York Lottery asks seven different bond brokers to quote a package of bonds that will pay each of the 25 future yearly payments. The Lottery buys the bonds from the broker with the best price for the complete package. An investment bank holds the bonds, and each year when one matures the funds are automatically placed in the New York Lottery's cash account. The funds are transferred to the prize payment account, and a check is written for the winner. Typically, the whole package of 25 bonds ends up costing the New York Lottery a little less than half of the jackpot amount.

However, most winners don't opt for annual payments. About 80% of winners choose the lump sum option, which is usually about half of the jackpot amount. Since the New York Lottery has to pay a lump sum to buy bonds anyway, it is just as happy to give that same amount of money to the winner instead. The Lottery goes through the process of getting quotations for the bonds, but instead of buying the bonds, it pays the winner the amount the bonds would have cost.

Calculating your winnings doesn't end here, though. Most U.S. lotteries take out 28% of the winnings to pay federal taxes. But, if your winnings were in the millions of dollars, you would be paying closer to 39.6% (the highest tax bracket) in federal taxes when tax time comes. Add state and local taxes, and you might end up with only half of your winnings when you are done paying taxes.

If you had opted for the lump sum prize in the $10 million lottery, the prize would be about $5 million. After federal and state taxes, you'd be left with about $2.5 million.

What if I had to file bankruptcy? What is the difference between chapter 7, 11, and 13?

When most of us think about a person who has filed bankruptcy, we imagine someone standing with his empty pockets turned inside out or possibly wearing a barrel, arms thrown up in despair. A cartoon bubble floats above his head filled with text that reads, "I've lost it all, even my last penny!" Although we can all get marks for a vivid imagination, this is not what happens, exactly. The severity of a person's situation actually depends on the type of bankruptcy he or she files. In most cases you don't find yourself stripped of all your possessions, relying on the kindness of friends or family members to take you into their home.

Title 11 of the United States Code (the Federal Bankruptcy Code) has four bankruptcy filings:

- Chapter 7 — Liquidation
- Chapter 11 — Reorganization
- Chapter 12 — Adjustment of Debts of a Family Farmer with Regular Annual Income
- Chapter 13 — Adjustment of Debts of an Individual with Regular Income

The filing generally depends on the person's financial situation. Because companies, married couples, and individuals are allowed to file chapter 7, this tends to be the most common filing.

A debtor filing chapter 7 is essentially scrapping everything and starting over, hoping for a clean financial slate. Basically, once the filing is underway, an administrator or trustee is appointed to maneuver the sale of the debtor's assets. This does not necessarily mean that everything the person owns is sold. Both federal and state laws allow for certain exemptions, meaning that the debtor might get to keep some property, such as his or her primary residence or personal items like clothing. Once the debtor's assets are liquidated, the trustee pays certain creditors a portion of the money raised. Obviously, not all of the creditors receive money from the proceeds, so many of those financial obligations are *forgiven*, or discharged. Once someone has filed for bankruptcy under chapter 7, he or she cannot file again for seven years, and debts that were not forgiven in a previous filing will not be discharged in the next filing.

It is important to note that the debtor will receive no forgiveness for certain debts. Alimony, child support, taxes, and student loans are almost never discharged under any bankruptcy filing. So, if a lot of your debt falls into these categories, you might be better off filing chapter 13.

Chapter 12 and chapter 13 are basically the same filing, except that chapter 12 is for family farmers and chapter 13 is for other individuals. As long as you have a steady, reliable income, less than $269,250 in unsecured debt (such as credit card debt) and less than $807,750 in secured debt (such as a mortgage or auto loan), you can file chapter 13. Once the filing is made, the debtor is assigned a trustee. The debtor and trustee develop a proposal for a repayment plan. The court decides whether to accept or alter the plan or dictate another repayment plan altogether. Once the plan is decided upon, it can last anywhere from 3 to 5 years.

You may be wondering why someone would file for chapter 12 or 13 instead of chapter 7. Here's why:

- Under chapter 12 and 13 filings, debtors do not have to liquidate their assets. Instead, they actually get to keep everything, not just the items that meet the legal exemption.

- In most chapter 12 and 13 cases, the debtor is repaying only a percentage of what he or she actually owes — sometimes as little as 30 cents to 50 cents on the dollar!

You hear about chapter 11 on the news all the time. Originally only intended for large corporations, individuals can now file chapter 11 as well. A chapter 11 bankruptcy is very similar to a chapter 13 bankruptcy. The main difference is that unlike chapter 13, chapter 11 has no limit regarding the amount of money owed by the debtor.

Filing for bankruptcy is not to be taken lightly. It affects your credit rating for many years. The decision to file is best made with the advice of a financial planner and/or a legal representative.

What if I have twins and want to send them to an Ivy League school? How much will I need to save each month?

A great number of people attending colleges and universities today rely on a combination of financial resources to cover their tuition and expenses, such as:

- Academic scholarships
- Athletic scholarships
- Financial aid
- Student loans

But what if you wanted to be able to send your children to school using only your own financial resources? Perhaps, because of your income, they would not qualify for financial aid. Or maybe you don't want them to be worried about competing for scholarships or fretting over paying back huge loans just after they graduate. How much money would you need to save?

Let's say that the twins are 3 years old. That gives you 15 years to save money for their college tuition and expenses. You've decided to save enough money so that your son can attend Cornell, your alma mater, and your daughter can go to Columbia, like your spouse. Currently, the cost of one academic year as a full-time student living on campus, including room and board and other expenses, is almost $35,000 at Cornell and a little over $35,000 at Columbia. Tuition and expenses will obviously be more 15 years from now. To project the anticipated costs, factor in an annual rate of increase of 6%. You see that you will need approximately $340,000 for a 4-year degree at Columbia and about $334,000 at Cornell. So, altogether, you will need about $674,000 for your children's tuition, and you have 15 years to come up with that money. How much will you have to put away each month?

You decide that you want the money somewhere you can get to it in the event there's an emergency. The local credit union offers a money market account with 5% interest. Using a basic compound-interest calculator (like the one found on our Web site: www.howstuffworks.com/interestcalc.htm) you discover that you need to save between $2,325 and $2,350 each month to afford the Ivy League schools. This is a lot of money to try to squirrel away, especially considering the money that you will be spending every day to raise the children!

Instead of Ivy League schools, you may want to consider a public university. This would cut your anticipated expenses to about $105,000 per twin — making your monthly savings payments a more reasonable $725 each month.

What if I were president of the United States? Would I be the highest paid person in the U.S.?

The answer to this question is a resounding no! From 1969 until recently, the president of the United States made $200,000 each year. In 1969 this could be considered an exceptionally good salary. At that time, the president made four and a half times more than a member of congress. Fast-forward to 1999, and the president was still making the same $200,000, while congressional salaries had grown from $42,500 to $136,700.

Obviously, the president's salary was due for a review. In 1999, proponents of a salary increase supported their arguments by suggesting that, were the increases of inflation applied since the last adjustment in 1969, the president would be earning more than $900,000. As a result, the president's salary was doubled. President George W. Bush makes $400,000 each year. But his salary doesn't come close to what some top executives are making.

Currently, over 500 CEOs of American companies garner salaries of $1 million or more annually. According to *Forbes* magazine, the salaries for the top five CEOs are as follows:

Dell Computer	Michael Dell	almost $236 million
Citigroup	Sanford Weill	about $216 million
AOL Time Warner	Gerald Levin	almost $165 million
Cisco Systems	John Chambers	about $157.5 million
Cendant	Henry Silverman	about $137.5 million

Although the presidential salary doesn't compare with these moguls of industry, it is more sizeable than what most Americans find themselves earning each year. The following (reported in *BusinessWeek* magazine) is a list of salaries, representing the national average for each occupation for the year 2000:

Accountant	$45,660
Administrative Assistant	$35,830
Computer Data Entry	$20,690
Computer Programmer	$49,900
Receptionist	$20,910
Truck Driver, Light	$21,440

Furthermore, according to the World Almanac, the median household income in the U.S. as of 1998 was $46,737. Reportedly 13% of all families brought in $100,000 or more, while at the other end, 10% did not even make the $16,661 required for a family of four to surpass the official poverty line.

What if I purchased ten shares of stock when Microsoft first went public?

This mega-company went public in March of 1986. At that time, the offering price for one share of stock was $21. If you were fortunate enough to get on board then, your initial investment of just $210 would be valued at just over $99,500 today! How is it possible that, in 16 years, $210 can grow to $99,500? To understand how this can happen, let's take a look at how stocks work.

Suppose that you want to start a business, and you decide to open a restaurant. You have $500,000, enough to buy the building and the equipment. At the end of your first year, here is what happened:

- You spent $250,000 on supplies, food, and the payroll for your employees.
- You add up all of the money you have received from customers and find that your total income is $300,000.

Since you have made $300,000 and paid out the $250,000 for expenses, your net profit is

$300,000 (income) – $250,000 (expense) = $50,000 (profit)

At the end of the second year, you bring in $325,000 and your expenses remain the same, for a net profit of $75,000. At this point, you decide that you want to sell the business. What is it worth?

One way to look at it is to say that the business is worth about $500,000. If you close the restaurant, you can sell the building, the equipment, and everything else and get $500,000. This is the asset value, or book value, of the business — the value of all of the business's assets if you sold them outright today.

However, if you keep the restaurant going, it will probably make at least $75,000 this year — you know that from your history with the business. Therefore, you can think of the restaurant as an investment that will pay out something like $75,000 in interest every year. Looking at it that way, someone might be willing to pay $1,500,000 for the restaurant and the prospect of earning a $75,000 yearly income. This would be a pretty sound investment because it represents a 5% rate of return:

interest income ÷ principal invested = rate of return

75,000 ÷ 1,500,000 = .05 or 5%

What if, instead of a single buyer, 10 people came to you and said, "Wow, I would like to buy your restaurant but I don't have $1,500,000." You might want to somehow divide your restaurant into 10 equal pieces and sell each piece for $150,000. In other words, you might sell shares in the restaurant. Then, each person who bought a share would receive one-tenth of the profits at the end of the year, and each person would have one out of ten votes in any business decisions. Or, you might divide ownership up into 3,000 shares, keep 1,500 for yourself, and sell the remaining shares for $500 each. That way, you retain a majority of the shares (and therefore the votes) and remain in control of the restaurant while sharing the profit with other people. In the meantime, you get to put $750,000 in the bank when you sell the 1,500 shares to other people.

Stock, at its core, is really that simple. It represents ownership of a company's assets and profits. A dividend on a share of stock represents that share's portion of the company's profits, generally dispersed quarterly or yearly.

Any business that wants to sell shares of stock to a number of different people does it by turning itself into a corporation. The process of turning a business into a corporation is called *incorporating*. By definition, a corporation has stock that can be bought and sold, and all of the owners of the corporation hold shares of stock in the corporation to represent their ownership. The company can either be privately held or publicly held. In a privately held company, the shares of stock are owned by a small number of people who probably all know one another. They buy and sell their shares among themselves. A publicly held company is owned by thousands of people who trade their shares on a public stock exchange.

When a corporation first sells stock to the public, it does it in an initial public offering (IPO), which is exactly what it sounds like: the first chance for the public to buy into a company, generally at a discounted price. The company might sell 1 million shares of stock at $20 a share to raise close to $20 million very quickly — the company won't get $20 million outright because a brokerage house will be handing the IPO, and that brokerage house will extract a fee from the sale. The company then invests the money it made from the IPO in equipment and employees. The investors (the shareholders who bought the $20 million in stock) hope that with the new equipment and employees, the company will make a profit and pay a dividend (a distribution of earnings to investors).

If a company traditionally pays out most of its profits to its shareholders, it is called an *income stock*. The shareholders get income from the company's profits. If the company puts most of the money back into the business, it is called a *growth stock*. The company is trying to grow larger, and ultimately increase value for the shareholders.

The price of an income stock tends to stay fairly flat. That is, from year to year, the price of the stock tends to remain about the same unless profits (and therefore dividends) go up or down.

Holders of growth stock do not get a yearly dividend, but they own a company whose value is increasing. Therefore, the shareholders can get more money when they sell their shares; someone buying the stock would see the increasing book value of the company and the increasing profit that the company is earning and, based on these factors, pay a higher price for the stock.

Sometimes, the shares of a company increase in value so much that the company itself or the stock market will decide that the valuation is simply too high for an average investor. When this happens, the stock *splits*. A stock split can be a 2 for 1 split, a 3 for 1 split, or even a 4 for 1 split or higher. Let's say you have 1 share of stock in a company and it is valued at $120. The company announces a 4 for 1 stock split. That means that you now have 4 shares instead of 1 and each is valued at $30. If the company then continues to increase in value, these shares could each rise to $120 and split again. You now would have 16 shares of stock (4 shares that each split into 4 more shares) worth $30 each — all from purchasing a single share of stock.

The IPO of Microsoft occurred in March of 1986. The stock has split eight times since that IPO. As a result of those splits, your original 10 shares would have grown into 1,440 shares today. The total return on your investment, since IPO, would be 47,317%.

What if I wrote a bad check?

No matter what the circumstance — whether done with intent or as a mathematical mishap — this can be quite a costly mistake. Although the fees and fines may vary slightly, the procedures for handling a bad check are basically the same at most banks and credit unions.

Suppose you go to the store to make a purchase. You write a $75 check, grab your bag, and go. Because of a math error, your check bounces. About a week or so later, you get a message from your bank that your account is overdrawn. You decide that it has to be a mistake and don't call back. About a week or so after that, you get a phone call from a collection agency, saying you owe them $125. The same day, you receive your bank statement with a letter stating that your account is overdrawn by $13, and that you must make a deposit to cover your overdraft immediately. Here's what happened:

1. You wrote the check.
2. The store submitted your check with its daily deposit.

3. Your check came up NSF (non-sufficient funds) and was returned to the store.

4. Your bank assessed a $29 NSF fee to your account.

5. The store received the NSF check back from the bank and presented your check once more, with another deposit.

6. Your check came up NSF again and was returned to the store.

7. Your bank assessed another $29 NSF fee to your account.

8. The store notified its collection agency.

Businesses and individuals that have been given an NSF check as payment actually have up to three chances to claim their money by presenting the check to the bank. However, most businesses don't choose to present a check more than once. They rely on a collection agency to recoup their money. In order to pay for the services of the collection agency, businesses charge their own NSF fee — usually something like $20 or $25. Because the check was presented to the bank twice, you not only receive a $29 NSF fee from your bank both times, but the store charged you its standard $25 returned-check fee twice. So, your initial payment of $75 ends up costing you $183 — that's a whopping additional $108.

Suppose two or three unrecorded transactions with your check card caused your overdraft. All of the additional NSF and returned-check fees can cause a domino effect, so that you could become several hundred dollars overdrawn very quickly.

It's not uncommon for a person to think, "Well, I'll show them — I'll stop using that account without ever paying up and eventually open one somewhere else." This is never a good decision. Banking institutions aren't fooled that easily. Once it's evident that you're not going to settle up, the bank notifies the credit bureau through an agency like Equifax or Check Systems. Your failure to pay will be noted on your credit report, where it will stay for 7 years. During this time, it will be utterly impossible for you to open another bank account. In addition, most banking institutions do not turn the other cheek. Even if you were to eventually go back to the bank to pay your debt, that bank would probably not reopen an account for you.

This entire scenario can be avoided. Today, many banks and credit unions offer something called *overdraft protection*. There are basically two types of protection from which to choose:

- The overdraft can be covered by transferring money from an attached account, such as a savings account.

- If you don't have another account, or a savings account, the overdraft can be covered by a line of credit — this is like applying for a loan that you may or may not need. You would apply for the loan through the overdraft protection program; if approved, the money would be available in the event it was needed.

The price of this type of protection is generally very minimal. Sometimes it's even free.

8

Breaking the Rules

What if I popped my knuckles all the time? • What if I looked straight at an eclipse of the sun? • What if I crossed my eyes for 10 minutes — would they really stick that way? • What if I went swimming right after I ate a really huge meal? • What if I touched dry ice? • What if I ate the contents of the little packet marked "do not eat" that you find in shoeboxes, vitamin bottles, and so on? • What if I put aluminum foil in the microwave? • What if I removed the tag from my mattress? • What if I didn't file and pay my income taxes? • What if I stopped paying my bills? • What if I stuck my finger in an electrical outlet? • What if I shot my television?

What if I popped my knuckles all the time?

If you've ever laced your fingers together, turned your palms away from you, and bent your fingers back and heard a loud crack or pop, you know what knuckle-popping sounds like. So, what would happen if you popped your knuckles all the time? Would it ruin your joints? Would it give you arthritis?

First, you need to know what happens inside your joints when you crack your knuckles. Joints produce that CRACK when bubbles burst in the fluid surrounding the joint. Joints are the meeting points of two separate bones, held together and in place by connective tissues and ligaments. All of the joints in your body are surrounded by *synovial fluid*, a thick, clear liquid. When you stretch or bend your finger to pop the knuckle, you cause the bones of the joint to pull apart. As they do, the capsule of connective tissue that surrounds the joint is stretched. By stretching this capsule, you increase its volume. With an increase in volume comes a decrease in pressure. So as the pressure of the synovial fluid drops, bubbles form through a process called *cavitation*. When the joint is stretched far enough, the pressure in the capsule drops so low that these bubbles burst, producing the pop that we associate with knuckle cracking.

It takes about 5 to 10 minutes for the gas to re-dissolve into the joint fluid. During this period of time, your knuckles will not crack. Once the gas is re-dissolved, cavitation can happen again, and you can start popping your knuckles again.

Does this cavitation do any damage? According to Anatomy and Physiology Instructors' Cooperative, only one in-depth study has been published. This study, done by Raymond Brodeur and published in the *Journal of Manipulative and Physiological Therapeutics,* examined 300 knuckle crackers looking for joint damage. The result: In general, if you pop your knuckles a lot, it can do some damage. There is no apparent connection between joint cracking and arthritis. However, habitual knuckle poppers did show signs of other types of damage, including soft-tissue damage to the joint capsule, a decrease in grip strength, and an increase in hand swelling. This damage is most likely a result of the rapid, repeated stretching of the ligaments surrounding the joint. A professional baseball pitcher experiences similar, although obviously heightened, effects in the various joints of his pitching arm.

On the positive side, there is evidence of increased mobility in joints right after popping. When joints are manipulated the muscles surrounding the joint relax. This is part of the reason why people can feel loose and invigorated after leaving the chiropractor's office, where cavitation is induced as part of the treatment. Backs, knees, elbows, and all other movable joints can pop just like knuckles do.

What if I looked straight at an eclipse of the sun?

You've probably heard that staring at the sun is bad for your eyes. The reason you've heard this is that people who stare at the sun can go blind. Here's why. When you were a kid, you may have performed the trick where you lit paper on fire using the sun and a magnifying glass. The light of the sun is so strong that, if you concentrate it with a lens, you can actually start a fire.

In your eye you have a lens. If you stare at the sun, this lens concentrates a spot of sunlight on your retina, and it burns it too. The light is so intense that it kills cells on your retina.

So much hype surrounds staring at a solar eclipse because, on a day-to-day basis, most folks know better than to stare up at the sun. The problem with a solar eclipse is that it is an extremely rare event. In fact, all of us here in the United States are going to have to wait until the year 2017 for the next solar eclipse (it's path of totality will run from the west coast of Oregon to the east coast of South Carolina). Because these eclipses hardly ever happen, everyone wants to see them when they do occur. People are tempted to do what they know they shouldn't, thinking that a few seconds of looking at the eclipse won't do any harm. Usually, they believe they are right, because no initial pain is associated with a retinal burn. Generally, it takes several hours for the symptoms to manifest, and by then the damage has already been done.

What if I crossed my eyes for 10 minutes — would they really stick that way?

"Don't cross your eyes — they'll stick that way!" That's something most of us have heard from our mothers at one time or another. Can they actually stick? Let's take a look at how your eyes work.

Your eyeballs are controlled by six muscles. When you look up, down, left, or right, the muscles attached to your eyeballs make this movement happen. When you cross your eyes, you are simply telling your muscles to move your eyes inward together. This is something you naturally do when you look at something that's very close to your face.

So was mom's warning just a ruse so you would stop tormenting your younger brother with another one of your gross-out maneuvers? The answer to that question is yes. Although crossing your eyes for an extended period of time might cause a temporary strain on your eye muscles, no medical evidence suggests that they would stick that way. You would most likely suffer from some eye spasms or twitches, and your eyes might feel a bit fatigued, but they would certainly return to normal within an hour or so.

What if I went swimming right after I ate a really huge meal?

The family picnic at the lake is quite conducive to this scenario. You've just downed a huge cheeseburger and you couldn't resist following that up with a hot dog and some potato salad. It's hot, and the cool, shimmering water is practically calling your name. As it turns out, "Don't go swimming for an hour after you eat" is a good piece of advice. If you do hop into the lake right after that big meal, you could develop cramps and you risk drowning.

The key to understanding the risk is knowing that your body will always work to take care of its energy needs. Conflicting needs can cause problems. If you have just eaten, the food in your stomach is being digested. During digestion, the stomach muscles are doing an incredible amount of work, so they need a lot of blood. Now you go swimming. The muscles in your arms and legs are doing a lot of work too, so they also need a lot of blood. Unfortunately, managing two big loads like this is more than your body can handle. There's just not enough blood and oxygen to accommodate both workloads, so your muscles start to cramp.

Muscle cramps on land aren't that bad — they're pretty uncomfortable, but not devastating. You simply take a timeout from what you're doing until the cramp goes away. Muscle cramps in the water are a different story. You can't just sit down and wait it out. If the cramping is really bad, you won't be able to stay above water.

So, if you give your body enough time — about an hour — to digest your food and decrease the workload of your stomach, you decrease your risk of cramps.

What if I touched dry ice?

Dry ice is frozen carbon dioxide. It has the very nice feature of sublimation — as it melts, it turns directly into carbon dioxide gas rather than a liquid.

If you ever have to handle dry ice, you want to be sure to wear heavy gloves, because a block of dry ice has a surface temperature of $-109.3°F$. The super-cold surface can easily damage your skin if you touch it directly.

It's actually a lot like if you were to touch the handle of a hot pot or pan without an oven mitt. If you did this for less than a second — so that you simply felt the heat and quickly pulled your hand away — then at most your skin would be a little red. However, if you were to grab hold of the handle tightly for a couple of seconds or more, chances are you would get a pretty nasty burn. The heat kills the skin cells.

It's the same with dry ice. Dry ice actually freezes your skin cells if you touch it. The resulting injury is very similar to a burn and should be treated with the same medical attention. For the same reason, you never want to taste or swallow dry ice. This would be like drinking something that is scalding hot, and you would risk damaging your mouth, throat, and part of your esophagus.

What if I ate the contents of the little packet marked "do not eat" that you find in shoeboxes, vitamin bottles, and so on?

What you would be consuming is most likely silica gel or some other *desiccant* — something that adsorbs (collects) and holds water vapor. These little packets are found in all sorts of products to help maintain quality.

Shipping can cause all kinds of atmospheric conditions and changes in temperature. Increased moisture can spoil or permanently damage many products. For example, if a bottle of vitamins contained any moisture vapor and was cooled rapidly, the condensing moisture would ruin the pills. You will find little silica gel packets in anything that would be affected by excess moisture or condensation.

Silica gel can adsorb about 40% of its weight in moisture and can take the relative humidity in a closed container down to about 40%. Once the gel is saturated, you can get rid of the moisture and reuse the silica gel by heating it to above 300°F.

Silica gel is nearly harmless, and that is why you find it in food products. Silica, which is actually silicon dioxide (SiO_2), is the same material found in quartz. The gel form contains millions of tiny pores that can adsorb and hold moisture — it is essentially porous sand.

While the contents of a silica gel packet are basically harmless, it would be a rather unpleasant experience to attempt to consume the silica crystals. The sole job of these tiny desiccants is to adsorb moisture. If you emptied a packet of the stuff into your mouth, the moisture would be wicked away from the sides and roof of your mouth, gums, and tongue — giving an entirely new and all-too-accurate meaning to the phrase "dry mouth." If the silica gel did happen to make it past your mouth — which is unlikely because you would probably be making every effort

to spit it out — you might suffer a few irritating side effects,
such as

- Dry eyes
- An irritated, dry feeling in your throat
- Aggravated, dry mucous membranes and nasal cavity
- An upset stomach or stomach discomfort

A theoretical question...

Just how many silica packets would it take to adsorb all the
water from someone's body? Let's use a 210-pound man as an
example. We know that 70% of a human body Is made up of
water — 70% of 210 pounds is 147 pounds of water. We also
know that silica gel can adsorb about 40% of its weight in moisture. So 10 pounds of silica gel are needed to adsorb 4 pounds
of water.

It turns out that it would take 367.5 pounds of silica gel to
adsorb 147 pounds of water. Since a single packet of silica gel
weighs 0.1 ounces, that means a 210-pound man would have to
consume 58,800 packets of silica gel.

What if I put aluminum foil in the microwave?

The microwave oven is one of the great inventions of the twentieth
century — you will find microwave ovens in millions of homes
and offices around the world. At one time or another, we've all
been told not to use metal products, especially aluminum foil,
when cooking with a microwave oven. Stories of incredible explosions and fires usually surround these ominous warnings. Why is
that? Let's take a look at how microwave ovens work to find out.

As incredible as microwave ovens are, the technology behind
them is fairly simple. Microwave ovens use microwaves to heat
food. Microwaves are radio waves. In the case of microwave
ovens, the commonly used radio wave frequency is roughly
2,500 megahertz (2.5 gigahertz). Radio waves in this frequency
range have an interesting property: Water, fats, and sugars absorb
them. When absorbed, they're converted directly into atomic
motion — heat. Microwaves in this frequency range have another

interesting property: Most plastics, glass, or ceramics do not absorb them. But what about metal?

The walls inside a microwave oven are actually made of metal. It turns out that a fairly thick piece of metal works a lot like a mirror. But instead of reflecting an image, it reflects microwaves. If you were to put food in a heavy metal pan and put it in the microwave, it would not cook. The pan would shield the food from the microwaves, so the food would never heat up.

Tiny sharp pieces and thin pieces of metal are a different story. The electric fields in microwaves cause currents of electricity to flow through metal. Substantial pieces of metal, like the walls of a microwave oven, can usually tolerate these currents without problem. However, thin pieces of metal, like aluminum foil, are overwhelmed by these currents and heat up very quickly. So quickly, in fact, that they can cause a fire. Plus, if the foil is crinkled so that it forms any sharp edges, the electrical current running through the foil will cause sparks. If these sparks hit something else in the oven, perhaps a piece of wax paper, you'll probably be reaching for the fire extinguisher.

While it is highly unlikely that a small piece of foil is going to cause your microwave oven to totally explode, it could cause a fire. So, it's a good idea to stick to plastic wrap, paper towels, and any other non-metal kitchen aids.

What if I removed the tag from my mattress?

Somewhere along the way, most of us have heard that we aren't supposed to remove the tags from our mattresses or pillows because it violates some kind of law. In fact, many mattresses still have tags that say something like, "It is unlawful to remove this tag!" Those tags that you find dangling from the end of pillows or at the foot of your mattress are actually there to protect you, the end user. The main reason for the tags is to let you know

- That you're buying a new, never-been-used product
- What the fill contents of the pillow or mattress are

According to the U.S. Code, it is only unlawful to remove the tag prior to the sale and delivery of a pillow or mattress to the final consumer. Title 15 — Commerce and Trade, Chapter 2, Subchapter V — Textile Fiber Products Identification, Section 70c — Removal of stamp, tag, label, or other identification Statute (a) Removal or mutilation after shipment in commerce states:

> "After shipment of a textile fiber product in commerce it shall be unlawful, except as provided in this subchapter, to remove or mutilate, or cause or participate in the removal or mutilation of, prior to the time any textile fiber product is sold and delivered to the ultimate consumer, any stamp, tag, label, or other identification required by this subchapter to be affixed to such textile fiber product, any person violating this section shall be guilty of an unfair method of competition, and an unfair or deceptive act or practice, under the Federal Trade Commission Act."

In case you can't find your copy of the U.S. Code, simply look at the tag in question. One of our pillow tags displayed the following text:

50910180K   C

UNDER PENALTY OF LAW THIS TAG NOT TO BE REMOVED EXCEPT BY THE
CONSUMER

————————

ALL NEW MATERIAL CONSISTING OF POLYESTER FIBER

————————

REGISTRY NO. PA-23841 (KY)

————————

Certification is made by the manufacturer that the materials in this article are described in accordance with the law.

Once you have purchased a pillow or mattress, it is your right as the "ultimate consumer" to remove the tag. You may want to hang on to the tags for future reference — especially if you have any allergies to certain materials.

What if I didn't file and pay my income taxes?

The American tax system is a huge machine with a tax code that seems more complex than rocket science. Many of us have come to dread April 15th because of its connection to the Internal Revenue Service (IRS). In fact, taxes have always left a sour taste

Breaking the Rules

in the mouths of American citizens. This national hatred for taxes dates back to the tax burden placed on the American colonies by Great Britain. Colonists were taxed for every consumer good, from tea and tobacco to legal documents. This "taxation without representation" led to many revolts.

While a revolt is not imminent today, many of us have imagined a more personal revolt. Have you ever wondered what exactly would happen if you failed to file and pay your taxes one year?

Although most Americans tend to think about the tax system and the IRS only as the month of April approaches, the tax process is actually never ending. By law, employers are required to withhold employment taxes from their employees' earnings. People who are self-employed are still responsible for withholding taxes from their own wages.

In fact, the income tax process begins when a person starts a new job. The employee and employer agree on compensation, which will be figured into the gross income at the end of the year. One of the first things an employee has to do when hired is fill out all of the tax forms, including a W-4 form. The W-4 form lists all of the employees withholding allowance information, such as the number of dependents and childcare expenses. The information on this form tells an employer just how much money it needs to withhold from a person's paycheck for federal income tax. The IRS suggests that you check this form each year, as your tax situation may change from year to year.

As the employer collects the withheld money, it deposits the money into an approved financial institution. A report is filed on a quarterly basis to notify the IRS of how much money has been withheld from each employee's salary. Another report is filed at the end of the year as well.

Now, let's say you decided not to file this year. As with any other agency that is owed money, the government would not be pleased at all. Initially, it would send you a letter notifying you of your forgetfulness. If you failed to respond, you would receive more letters. Eventually the government would send a final letter, but this time it would include a bill. It turns out that the government has a right to determine what your income would be based on past records. This is known as a *Substitute for Return*, or SFR.

Let's say you were in a higher tax bracket during your last filing, but since then, you were laid off and had to take a considerable pay cut to find work. If the government bases its assessment on your previous employment, your bill would be much higher than it otherwise should be. Even if, for example, your job remained the same, with similar earnings, most SFRs include only the standard deductions. Any other deductions that you may be entitled to claim will not be included. Furthermore, there are penalties and fines associated with failure to file and failure to pay charges. These penalties can be as much as 50% to 75% of the original amount owed.

Once the government has sent you a bill, you have two options:

- You pay the taxes (even if it's an overpayment). You can go to tax court later to protest the amount and refile, this time including the appropriate deductions and so on.

- You decide not to pay at all.

If you continue to pursue your personal revolt against taxation, it could cost you even more. The government has the right to recoup its money as it sees fit. It can

- Place a levy on your bank account.

- Place a lien on your home.

- Seize your car, boat, or any other personal or real property of value.

Simply put, failure to file, failure to pay, and tax evasion can result in any number of civil and even criminal punishments, including imprisonment.

What if I stopped paying my bills?

Not paying your bills on time can affect your credit rating, plain and simple. There is little that people can do in life without credit, and even less if they have bad credit. Good credit is like a key. It's what allows you to get a loan from the bank for college, a new car, or a new home. In many companies, it is customary to check the credit of prospective employees before they are hired as one check of their reliability. If you are a credit risk, you might be an employment risk as well.

If you've ever paid a bill late, you've probably noticed that you are charged a fine. If it has happened more than once with the same company, what you might not have noticed, or even known, is that in addition to the extra charge, your tardiness was reported to the credit bureau. Procedure varies from company to company, but as little as two late payments can result in a mark on your permanent financial record. If being slightly behind can tarnish your credit report, imagine what not paying your bills at all can do.

As soon as it is evident that you don't intend to pay your bill, the company will turn its information over to a collection agency — this can be an outside agency or a division within the affected company. Once this happens, the collection agency will start by calling you. Agents will call you at home, at work, and even at a relative's house, if they can locate the appropriate phone number. After they contact you, if you still do not pay up, the collection agency can turn the matter over to the courts.

Fortunately for you, unless the agency has an adequate claim that you were fraudulent in some manner, it cannot have you sent to jail immediately. Usually a judgment will be granted and the collection agency, on behalf of the company to whom you owe money, will be able to do any or all of the following to recover the money:

- Garnish your salary (up to 50%).
- Seize personal property such as cars, boats, or jewelry.
- Place a lien on your bank account.

Although regulations differ from state to state, the collection agency might even be able to seize your home. Most states have a homestead exemption, which allows people to maintain their property, if the property doesn't pass a certain value. But many of these values are only modest. If your home is valued beyond this allowance, you can be forced to vacate and your home will be sold to help pay your debt. At this point, even after you make amends and cover the full amount owed, this indiscretion will stay on your credit report for as many as 7 or even 10 years.

What if I stuck my finger in an electrical outlet?

Many people, parents in particular, really wonder what would happen if someone — possibly their child — were to stick his or her finger in an electrical outlet. According to the U.S. Consumer Product Safety Commission, each year an estimated 3,900 people find themselves in the emergency room seeking treatment for injuries caused by accidents involving electrical outlets. About a third of these patients are children who decided to stick some kind of metal object (such as a paper clip or spoon handle) or a finger into the outlet. This number may seem high, but these people are actually the lucky ones. There are hundreds of folks who never make it to the emergency room.

If you stick your finger in an electrical outlet, the current can maim or even kill you. It turns out that the human body is an excellent conductor for electricity. Electricity is always looking for a quick and simple path to the ground. Because about 70% of a human body is made up of water, it is extremely easy for electricity to course through you in a matter of seconds. At a minimum, electric shock can cause

- Headache
- Muscle fatigue or spasms
- Temporary unconsciousness
- Temporary breathing difficulty

Some of the more serious and possibly fatal side effects of electrical shock are

- Severe burns at point of contact and along the electricity's course through the body
- Vision loss
- Hearing loss
- Brain damage
- Respiratory arrest or failure
- Cardiac arrest (heart attack)
- Death

If someone nearby does stick fingers or some kind of metal object into an outlet and receives an electrical shock, DO NOT touch the person. If you touch him or her, the electricity can move from that person's body into yours, shocking you both in the process. You should quickly shove the victim away from the outlet using an object that does not conduct electricity. A chair, broom handle, or dry towel will work. Once contact has been broken, quickly check the victim's breathing and pulse and look for burns. The person should seek medical help immediately.

What if I shot my television?

Every now and again as you're driving down the freeway, you will see that famous bumper sticker that says "Shoot Your Television." And many times as you're watching television, the thought of a well-placed shot may cross your mind. Whether it's a bad game for the home team, a bad sitcom, or a bad commentator spouting off about something else, there are lots of reasons to kill the tube.

What if you did actually take it out back and shoot it? We are, of course, talking about a standard television with the huge glass picture tube, so there is something big and meaty to aim at. TVs in the 25-inch and greater range have a massive piece of glass that weighs between 50 and 100 pounds.

Here at HowStuffWorks headquarters we actually tried this experiment.

Since it is a *vacuum* tube, there's been a lot of discussion in the urban legend community about a massive implosion that would occur when the bullet first cracked the glass. The idea is that the vacuum would suck the glass fragments in, and then they would rebound at shrapnel speed.

At least when we tried it here, nothing like that happened. The bullet went in very cleanly, punched a very neat hole through the glass, and air quickly filled the tube through that hole. There certainly was not an implosion.

After you've taken the shot, there's no good reason not to take the whole thing apart and explore the interior. So that's what we did. A hammer cracked away the rest of the glass, and here's what was inside:

- **The front glass.** The front glass is an extremely thick, sturdy piece of work. It is actually leaded crystal, like optical glass, so that it has great clarity and consistency. The front piece contains between 1% and 2% lead.

- **The phosphor.** On the back of the glass is a phosphor coating. It is a white powder that flakes off.

- **The shadow mask.** Right behind the screen is the shadow mask. You don't need the mask in a black-and-white TV, but in a color TV you need it because there are three electron guns and three different colors of phosphor on the screen. At each pixel on the screen there are tiny dots of red, green, and blue phosphor, and the mask makes sure that the right electron gun aligns with the right dot. The most common way to make the shadow mask is to take a thin piece of metal and punch hundreds of thousands of incredibly tiny holes in it.

- **The electron gun.** At the back of the tube is the electron gun. Once you chip it out, it's a very elegant looking piece of metal and ceramic. Three things happen in the gun: Filaments at the back of the gun heat up to produce the electrons, then the electrons get accelerated, and then they get focused into a tight beam. When the electron beams (three of them, in a color TV) leave the electron gun, the electrons are moving at about a third of the speed of light. That gives them enough energy to light up the phosphor when they hit it.

So that's what you would find if you actually shot your television. It's probably not an experiment that you need to repeat, because what you end up with is 50 pounds of leaded glass fragments all over the yard, and it makes a big mess!

Index

sweating and not bathing, 50–51

swimming after eating, 118–119

synovial fluid, 116

T

taxes, income, 123–125

taxes on lottery winnings, 104

television, shooting at, 128–129

temperature
  outer space conditions, 6
  wildfires and, 25

tesla, 72

time zones, 74

topography, wildfires and, 25

transportation in domes, 31

trash production of humans, 32

trees, falling into, 2

truck driver's salary, 109

tuition, 107–108

twenty-five cents saved every day, 102–103

2001: A Space Odyssey, 7

U

unconscious state, outer space and, 6

underground water, 80

underwater, driving, 38–39

United States Geological Survey, 80

unleaded fuel vehicles, diesel fuel in, 36–37

U.S. Code, 122–123

U.S. Defense Advanced Research Projects Agency (DARPA), 48

U.S. Environmental Protection Agency, 16

U.S. president's salary, 108–109

U.S.Consumer Product Safety Commission, 127

V

vacuum tube, 128

Valdez, Alaska, 20

vitamins, 58

W

W-4 form, 124

walk-in freezers, 86–89

wallets, stolen, 93–96
  prevention, 95
  reporting, 96

water, 59
  drinking, 90–91
  falling into, 2
  in gas, 36
  from Hoover Dam escaping, 22
  icebergs as source of, 17–18
  infected with bacteria, 26–27
  on moon, 10
  needed for two years, 9